POWER GLASS

PERSONAL ESSAYS

KATHERINE COOPER

To my husband, Gene, who always believes in me.

To my nieces and nephews, Evie, Ellie, Logan, Luke, and Ruby. May my generation leave a better society for you.

CONTENTS

ACKNOWLEDGEMENTS

Thank you to all the women who came before me. To call you an "inspiration" is insufficient.

Thank you, Mom, for instilling in me a love of reading and language. That appreciation directly led to writing this book. Thank you also for your bravery. Even though you didn't complete your degree at Virginia Tech, the fact that you were one of the first women who walked those halls served as an inspiration to me. You motivated me to take a stand in male territory.

Thank you, Grandma Cooper and Grandma Campbell. I know your lives weren't easy, either. You experienced World Wars, the Great Depression, and so many other unnamed hardships. Yet you survived. Thank you, also, to my great-grandmothers and all of the female ancestors who came before me. Your bravery is in my genes.

Thank you to my sisters, Morgan, Sarah, and Nancy. I'm not sure if you realize how much you inspire me. Each of you has been faced with challenging experiences and has had to make difficult choices. Every time you are challenged, you rise to the occasion. Whether it's quitting a job that is no longer fulfilling to stay home with your children, moving to the U.S. Virgin Islands to find work and making a home in this new place, or starting your own business empowering women, my sisters never cease to amaze me.

I've been truly blessed in my education and career to find amazing women who have become my friends. In no particular order, thank you, Miranda Donovan, Ida Barksdale, Alex Greif, Becky Folk, Nicole Pulido, Lauren Duda, Lindsay Hussey, Laura McGlinchey, Mary Willis, Christy Mollet, Angele Dugas, Amy Flower, Holly Millard-Burns, Carol Sizemore, Adriana Camargo,

Yelin Suh, Nicole Bradley, Leanne Phillips, Katie Pehrson, Julia Yard, Chelsea Hadsel, and many more. Thank you for your friendship and your encouragement, especially on the rough days.

Thank you, Dr. Allison Baski. You pushed me to do my best. You were hard on me, but I know that you wouldn't have been so if you hadn't believed I was capable. You believed in my capability more than I did.

Thank you, Dad, for being happy I was a girl. Thank you for showing me car parts when you were repairing cars in our driveway and for encouraging me (even if it wasn't direct) to go into STEM and become an engineer. You taught me that I could be whatever I wanted to be.

Thank you to all the men I've worked and gone to school with who treated me as competent, smart, and valuable to the team. A special thank you to Kevin Middleton, Matt Sievert, Andre Clayborne, Travis Phillips, Tom Herbert, Joe Moore, Ravi Jha, Brian Powell, and Bill Rogers. There are many more, unnamed.

Thank you, Candi Cross. You saw the potential in my (very rough) first draft and helped mold it into this book. I cannot overstate how much I appreciate the hours you put in to make this book the *powerful* manuscript it became.

Lastly, thank you to my husband, Gene. You've always been in my corner. I love you.

CORRIDORS OF POWER

"The power to question is the basis of all human progress."

—INDIRA GANDHI

AN ELEPHANT CAN carry 14,000 pounds. The anaconda squeezes with the power of ten men. An eagle carries four times its weight. But a dung beetle lifts 1,141 times its weight. If these creatures knew the full scale of their power!

Do you consider yourself powerful? How do you define, measure, and exercise power? Have you used your power for good or for ill intent? Are you hungry for more power? Why?

This isn't an interrogation but rather, an invitation to think about power distinctly from other elements that we human beings tend to rank and rate ourselves on freely and openly such as money, material things, physical weight, age, the zip code we live in, and the zip code we want to live in. No doctor, therapist, mentor, or partner asks us about our relationship to power and how it is impressed upon our life and others. However, I think about power a lot.

Trigger Warning: This book explores *power* and its mirror side, *fragility*, in the vivid color of experiences, philosophical musings, facts, and change theory.

POWER

- Strength
- Intelligence
- Capability
- Curiosity
- Freedom
- Resilience
- Sexuality
- Confidence
- Awareness
- Fearlessness
- Ally

fragility

- violence
- ridicule
- inadequacy
- unemployment
- entrapment
- enemies
- shame
- subordination
- minimization

It's easy, even humorous and entertaining, to examine the power struggles between 8.7 million species we live on the planet with. The power of people is a different story with infinite glass ceilings to patiently chip away at or hysterically shatter. But since women's representation in politics directly correlates to policy and the creation of laws that govern, along with prosperity, the gauge of balance and power in this space is paramount.

Women's representation in politics globally continues to increase, albeit slowly, according to new data from CFR's "Women's Power Index," an interactive tool first published in February 2020 that ranks 193 UN member countries on their progress toward gender parity in political participation.

It's worth noting that three countries have made significant progress toward gender parity in political representation since the Index was updated. In the wake of the 2020 election, the United States featured the largest improvement in its score and ranking, moving from #128 to #43. As President Joe Biden sought to fulfill his campaign pledge to appoint a gender-balanced cabinet, the number of women cabinet members rose from 17 percent to nearly half (47%), with two cabinet vacancies still remaining. The number of female members in U.S. Congress rose to a record-breaking 27%. Across the Atlantic, in Brussels, a historic cabinet composed of eight women and six men under Prime Minister Alexander De Croo helped Belgium leap ahead in the rankings, from #32 to #13. And in Lithuania, Ingrida Simonyte, the newly elected female prime minister, appointed a nearly gender-balanced cabinet, which boosted the country's score and ranking to #29. Once again, Costa Rica and Rwanda sit at the top of the rankings, demonstrating how gender quotas and reservations make a powerful difference in elevating women's leadership.

Twenty-two countries are now led by women, an achievement reached only once before, in 2019. I'm happy to see the power scale slowly tipping in global leadership, for I believe the quality of our lives and future generations is at stake. For the purpose of crystal clarity, I will depict *my* story of power and fragility, starting with my own industry: nuclear power. And it's pretty damned powerful, with its history dating back thousands of years.

Writing for International Atomic Energy Agency (IAEA), Daria Shumilova and Irena Chatzis depict Tatjana Jevremovic, a trailblazing nuclear engineer at the IAEA, who is known for developing a seminal neutronics code that, years later, is still used in Japan for relicensing nuclear power plants. Growing up in the Serbian capital, she was always fascinated by books, dictionaries, science magazines—anything that imparted knowledge. She wrote poems, started to paint and read voraciously. One day, when she was about twelve, she came across a book called *On Nuclear Energy* by Donald J. Hughes and translated by Dragoslav Popovic, who later became her professor at the University of Belgrade.

Then and there, she decided to study nuclear engineering and chose it as her profession. Her parents were less enthusiastic, for reasons I'm sure many parents of female students in the sciences can sympathize with. She applied to the Faculty of Electrical Engineering at the University of Belgrade, which, that year, admitted eighty students. Only thirteen ended up graduating, seven of them women, including Jevremovic. In percentages, that's roughly 54 percent female representation in that graduating class. Contrast that to the roughly 20 percent female contribution to engineering degrees in many U.S. universities.

Her contributions are the construct of a type of power that I wish we were all wired to harness and fuse together for humankind above and beyond other types of power addressed herein. She has published over 200 scientific papers, overseen the graduation of more than sixty students in nuclear engineering, and authored numerous technical reports. I want to be like her. In fact, I am like her. But our lives are defined by different chapters. An archive of power and fragility.

CHAPTER 1
SEX

INSTANT MESSENGER FROM HELL

"Violence is the last refuge of the incompetent."

—Isaac Asimov

DESPITE MY ACADEMICALLY charged brain, I ended up spending five years in college because I failed thermodynamics, a branch of physics, in my junior year. The reason I failed was that I was clinically depressed and could barely tumble out of bed every day. I was skipping classes; I just didn't care anymore. The reason I was depressed was that I had been raped.

I had been raped.

It seems so blunt and matter-of-fact seeing the words typed on the screen: "*I had been raped.*" I mull them over as I re-read them. The feeling they bring is anything but "blunt and matter-of-fact." No emotion attached? That is far from accurate. Being raped fundamentally changed the relationships with the people in my life and sent me into a tailspin. The relevance to the rest of this story—and my broader story—is multi-fold. Firstly, it was the women in my life at the time who were the ones I felt most betrayed by. Secondly, I was made painfully aware of rape culture with a front-row seat to the event itself and the aftermath. Thirdly, it made me aware that as a woman in our society, we will always be judged (and found wanting) for everything we do.

With today's #MeToo movement, we're seeing a sense of solidarity with women. But back in the early 2000s, there was still a lot of blame going on. People always say things like "If she was really raped, why wouldn't she press charges? Why wouldn't she tell someone?" Well, after having been through the whole process, I can tell you why. Plain and simple, it's because survivors are forced to relive the rape event over and over and over again through interviews at the hospital, discussions with the police, and creepy outpourings of questions from "well-meaning" friends. Then there's the people who won't look you in the eyes anymore, who are awkward around you, never know what to say around you, and just stop being your friend because cutting you out of their life is easier than figuring out how to talk about this painful event that happened to someone they cared about. It is a horrible existence, and in the end, you cut contact with everyone you can who is a reminder of that time—except your family, and we'll come to that later.

To understand how the women in my life let me down, you need to know the story from the beginning. This is the first time I have told this story since telling it to the police, and the first time I've given all the details because they were so mortifying that I couldn't even tell the hospital staff or the police when they interviewed me. I have finally gotten to the point where I can review the story without feeling physically ill. But it will never be expunged.

Back in the late 90s and early 2000s when it was still the early age of the Internet, everyone was "online." Now, we're on phone apps, and it's a much broader landscape to plow and pillage in. There were instant messaging apps and there were people all over the globe chatting on them. AOL Instant Messenger was really popular, as was a service called ICQ (I Seek You). As I think back to the name of that latter app, using the hard-earned wisdom of another twenty-some years, I think how creepy and downright stalkerish it is. I wonder how many other girls rue the day they came across those apps.

I was one of the people chatting my heart out and enjoying the novelty of invisibility. An awkward teenager who didn't always feel she came across well in person, I could be anyone, and say anything online. We see this in the extreme now with social media bullying. But this was a much different context.

I was chatting with several men at the time. Some were relatively harmless, like one friend I made online, who I will call Melvin. Others were pervy, old men and I should have known better. I thought I was safe in my college apartment halfway across the country from some of these creeps, but the creep never did really wash off. I was a rebel, a teenager experiencing her sexuality for the first, or in actuality, second time. I was woefully unprepared, especially since, like a lot of young women, I equated love with a man's desire to have sex with me.

I lacked confidence as a girl. I was always overweight—sometimes by a little; other times, by a lot—and never learned to love my body the way some plus-size women do. Only now, at the heaviest I've been (like weight is a number we wear on our shirts for all to see, a name tag of digits that identifies us) am I finally close to that self-love that I admire and find beautiful in so many other plus-size beauties.

My "boyfriend," who I lost my virginity to, was my coworker at a major amusement park in Virginia. (Readers must guess which one, as the park probably wouldn't relish that particular detail being shared!) We were sixteen years old, and he was a cute African American guy. Seeing hearts and stars in the runup to the special event, I thought I was in love. I'd never been touched by a man before. I had no idea how good being sexually aroused could and did feel. Then I met "Michael." Soon, with labored breath and soft giggles, I permitted him to touch me in ways I'd never imagined. I handed my virginity to him on a platter in a storage shed in the back lot of a funnel cake shack. Yeah (*facepalm*). With all this hoopla, didn't he love me? What did I know about love? So, my inaugural sexual experience seriously lacked elegance and longevity.

Michael disappeared rather quickly. I felt desperate for someone else to think I was pretty, sexy, desirable.

I always felt like the outsider in all my social groups. In college, I wanted so much to fit in, to find that mythical group of friends that was always portrayed in books and film. The friends you could always call on. The ones—male or female— that you sat snuggled with on the sofa, eating popcorn, and binging movies. I never found that comfort. I always felt like I said the wrong thing, was teased even by people who said they were my friends. So, was it wrong for me to want one person who saw me? I mean really *saw me*. Saw how funny I was, how generous of heart, how loving?

One of the men I chatted my heart out to was a Ph.D. student at a major Virginia university, where I was earning my B.S. in mechanical engineering. He was Turkish and intriguing. I admit flirting with him was an act of rebellion. My family was very conservative, and this was during a period of unrest in the Middle East. What better way to flout my parents' authority? Rebellious or not, I didn't deserve what happened to me.

One hot, thick word led to another until we soared beyond flirting. I informed him that I was a virgin because it seemed to up his thermometer of interest in me, and besides, I wasn't all that proud of the funnel cake shack. He insisted that he would be my "first." I know, I know! *Red alert! Red alert!* I wish I could go back and shake this girl now. But I do not blame her for her gullibility. There have been many more experienced women that have fallen into the same trap. And they didn't deserve what happened to them either.

I invited him over to watch a movie. We watched *The Game*, a thriller starring Michael Douglas, and to this day, I can't watch anything with Douglas in it without cringing. I went to see *Avengers Endgame* and had to avert my gaze during the parts in which he had cameos. I didn't see much of the movie "that night." That's still how I refer to it: "that night." So, you'd think it wouldn't have bothered me much, but it's funny the things that stick with you.

I thought two of my roommates were home. They were art students and spent a lot of time in one of their bedrooms smoking pot, so I felt relatively safe with a strange man in the apartment. By the time I realized they weren't home, it was too late.

When I opened the door and saw him, something in my brain told me to shut the door and tell him to go away. In that order. But I suppressed it because I was a shy kid, and I was used to feeling uncomfortable around new people. I invited him in, we sat down, and we started watching the movie. I don't remember any conversation except for the conversation snippets entangled in the assault. Maybe there was small talk, but if so, it got erased from my mind because of what occurred.

I don't even remember if we kissed. I don't think we did. Here is what I do remember: I remember him pulling his penis out of his pants. I remember it being the ugliest penis I had ever seen. Not that I'd seen a collection or variety by that point, having a pretty sheltered teenage life. And not that any penis is attractive; sorry male readers: I know most of you think your penis is the sexiest thing on the planet (that's why so many of you think dick pics are so thrilling for women). I remember his ugly penis being already fully erect. I remember that he took a drop of pre-ejaculate from the tip of his penis and put it inside my mouth and rubbed it around. Thinking about that still makes me want to gag.

I remember that I mumbled, "No." I remember that instead of heeding my response, he pulled my head into his lap and choked me with his penis, using my long hair like a handle to hold my head in his lap. Later, I thought, *maybe he didn't hear me. Maybe he didn't know I didn't want it.* But I don't really believe that was true.

I remember still being convinced my roommates were there and not wanting them to walk out and see us like that. All I wanted was for this to be over so he would leave; if I gave him what he wanted, he would go away. How many women have thought the same thing in similar circumstances? I remember that I took him to my bedroom. I remember that he bent me over the side of my bed, pulling up my long skirt, pulling down my panties, and penetrating me from behind.

Thank God he penetrated my vagina. I don't know what I would have done if he'd invaded me anally. And in retrospect, thank God that he penetrated me with his penis and not some other object. In a lot of ways, it could have been much, much worse. Note: I have been made to explore such worst-case scenarios, nonsensical comparisons to other rape scenarios, to detract from the fact that I was raped. There is a book by Roxane Gay called *Not* That *Bad: Dispatches from Rape Culture,* which explores the spectrum of rape and sexual assault. It is a potent reminder for all of us that, no matter the circumstances of our assaults, it is *that* bad.

I remember that he entered me repeatedly, working towards his orgasm. I remember that he told me to scream for him.

That is officially all I remember of the event, although some nagging feeling tells me he raped me twice. Maybe there's a reason I don't remember the other time. Maybe my brain is doing me a favor, like brains do for many trauma survivors.

You'd think in a traumatic event like this that every occurrence would be seared into your brain. However, your brain doesn't work like that in survival mode.

I don't remember my rapist leaving.

I wasn't drinking that night. I was wearing a long-sleeved sweater and a long skirt. I invited him over to my place because what location is safer for a date than your own house? And still, I was raped. Should I have known better than to flirt with him, to invite him to my house? Maybe, probably, but how many other women have flirted with a man at a bar and brought him back to their place, only to find out that wasn't the "right thing" to do?

This exposes one of the major fallacies of our lives. We are taught that if we do the right things (don't drink too much, don't stay out too late, don't wear clothes that are too revealing, don't draw too much attention to yourself; funny how this seems more like not doing the wrong things versus doing the right things), then we will be safe. But that, dear readers, is a lie. It is possible to do everything right and still have something this bad happen to you. That's why society has to find something wrong in what we did, and it's why women can be so unbelievably harsh on rape and sexual assault survivors. We need to believe that we're safe if we do the right things. We need it on a level that is indescribable.

DNA LIBRARY

*"People are like stained glass windows. They sparkle and
shine when the sun is out, but when the darkness sets in, their
true beauty is revealed only if there is a light from within."*

—Elisabeth Kubler-Ross

To say that you're among the hundreds of thousands of people who
have your identifying info on a rape kit is deeply disturbing. Someone overpowered you. Someone violated you. But the kit also means
that you at least reported it to someone, and then, by default, at
least a handful of people know. I should add that thousands upon
thousands of unexamined rape kits are, at this moment, piled up in
warehouses around the country. What an outrage. What a slap in
the face for survivors and a victory for those who are lurking around
corners, unpunished.

I want to personally thank Martha Goddard for beginning a
revolution in forensics by envisioning and creating the first stan-
dardized rape kit, containing items like swabs and combs to gather
evidence, and envelopes to seal it in for the purpose of bringing
criminals to justice. However, I wish I had never come across it.
I wish we didn't live in a world where rape kits are necessary, and
much less where I'm actually grateful that such an item was created.
What a terrible social commentary.

I sat on my twin-size bed, wrapped in a blanket, after my
rapist left. I don't know how long I sat that way. After a while,

when I came out of my shocked state, I called someone. I'll call him "Geoff." He was a poor choice as an "outcry witness," otherwise known as the first person that someone tells after they've been raped. Geoff was emotionally immature, had never even had sex, and was incapable of dealing with this. After he literally told me that he couldn't help me, and after I cried some more, I called Melvin (yes, the same Melvin that I had met online). Melvin called my parents, who called my uncle, and that's how I ended up at the ER for my first-ever pelvic exam at the age of nineteen. This pelvic exam was performed as part of the rape kit.

With the intent of speaking to a general audience here, let's talk about what a pelvic exam entails. Under normal, healthy circumstances, the pelvic exam is part of a woman's gynecological annual. When facilitated for a rape kit, it's like all familiarity goes out the door.

The vagina is a stretchable (to a certain extent), muscular canal, but for a physician to look inside it and see a woman's cervix, they have to open it. Your legs are up in stirrups, you're in the so-called "birthing position," your entire pelvic area is exposed for the world to see (or at least the small subset that seems to be crawling up your vagina during the exam). They use a device called a "speculum" to widen your vagina so that they can perform the exam. A speculum gets inserted and then cranked open with a mechanism something like a clamp in reverse. Instead of being squeezed by hand to close it down on whatever you are trying to glue together, the squeezing opens the speculum, widening the vaginal canal so the cervix is visible.

This hurts! No, women don't get off having a speculum squeezed inside of us, as some men fantasize. We do like some things inserted in our vagina, by our choice, our desire. Yes, the doc or assistant slathers lube on the speculum, but it doesn't somehow smooth the rough edges of the plastic or metal (much like a man fingering a woman when he has badly trimmed fingernails). The vagina, despite its primary function as a birth canal, is very tender and sensitive.

After the speculum is implanted and opened, the doctor reaches in with a long Q-tip-looking thing (think DNA swab or strep test swab). Then the scraping, which feels like sandpaper, on your cervix. This sensation inside your vagina is foreign, wrong. It is incredibly uncomfortable, but if the doctor is efficient and has decent aim, the action is expedient. Then they insert two fingers inside (again, this does not feel good) and they press very firmly on the ovaries and uterus to see if they can palpate anything between the fingers inside you and the hand on your lower abdomen. That part hurts the most, ironically.

So, at nineteen, after a rape, I got to experience this for the first time. It was like being violated all over again.

Since my rapist forced oral sex on me, my mouth was swabbed for DNA. The purpose of the vaginal swab, normally used to check for HPV and abnormal cervical cells during a routine pap smear performed during a pelvic exam, was to swab for DNA from my vagina. My nails were scraped. My body was swabbed. All while I told the story to multiple people who paraded through the exam room.

That's also where I received the morning-after pill, a massive dose of hormones, similar hormones to those in the birth control pill. It keeps the egg from implanting on the uterine wall. It does not keep the sperm from fertilizing the egg. The consequence of the hormone dosage is that it makes you horribly nauseated (not nauseous, as some say; "nauseous" means "to make one ill," not the feeling of being ill).

Now that twenty years have passed, I am grateful for those few days of nausea because the alternative could have been worse. I could have ended up pregnant with his baby. I know myself well enough to know that I would have terminated the pregnancy. Having one's rapist's baby is far different from having a baby, even from an unplanned pregnancy that results from a consensual sexual experience. Not to mention in the state of Virginia, he would also have had parental rights. To be clear, my rapist could have been able to sue me for custody of the child had I gotten pregnant and carried it to term. How fucked up is that?

I want to pause here and say that I admire any woman who voluntarily carries her rapist's baby to term and either places the baby up for adoption or keeps it. (*Involuntarily* is a separate issue that earns heartfelt compassion.) I know women who have done this, and I cannot put into words my awe at their strength. I want to be clear, too, that I do not sit in judgement of women who decide to carry a baby that is a product of rape to term. Nor do I sit in judgement of those who made a similar decision to mine. I've done many things that I would not want to be judged for, so I do not judge this. We make our own decisions and deserve the respect and compassion of others (though we don't often get it) for these decisions.

It takes up to seven days for an egg to be fertilized. Sperm can live up to seven days in the vagina and uterus. So, even if you have consensual sex, it's not like you know you're pregnant the next day. A lot of advertisements make you believe that all women stop their periods after the egg implants in the uterus. That is simply not true. Some women have periods all the way through their pregnancies. Typical "wisdom" (and I use the term loosely) says that a woman doesn't know she's pregnant until she misses a period. But what if she doesn't realize she's pregnant for six or eight or twelve weeks? That happens more often than people like to admit.

Again, looking back, I know that if I had found that I was pregnant six or eight or twelve weeks later, I would not have been able to carry that baby to term. I was so depressed. I considered killing myself. I lost most of the friends that I thought I had. Being pregnant on top of everything else…. It is said that "God does not give one more than they can handle." But what we like to forget is that what we can handle often involves more pain than we really want to experience. I didn't want to experience the pain I went through. I don't want to still be experiencing it. But I guess I "handled" it (more on that later).

RIPPLE EFFECTS

"The relationship between parents and children, but especially between mothers and daughters, is tremendously powerful, scarcely to be comprehended in any rational way."

—JOYCE CAROL OATES

Rape is a traumatic experience. It causes fear, rage, anxiety, and post-traumatic stress disorder (PTSD). It seems obvious that rape and sexual assault would have a lingering mental, emotional, and, yes, spiritual effect on the rape survivor. Shows like *Law and Order: SVU* have gone a long way towards normalizing these impacts (how awful that these acts happen often enough to need *normalization*). But we seldom think about the effect these acts have on the family and friends of the victim. These acts, perpetrated on loved ones, may be triggering, as one remembers their own assault or near brush with assault. How many women experience "rape precursors" even if they don't experience the full act? Are those precursor activities any less traumatizing?

Rape can also provoke feelings of rage and powerlessness in the spouse or partner of the survivor of rape. These individuals, the closest relationship to the experiencer of the rape or assault, may not know how to channel those feelings. Why wasn't I there? Could I have prevented this? Why would someone hurt the person I love in this manner?

In this way, rape and sexual assault are like a rock thrown in a pond. The survivor's experience is the central ripple, while the ever-expanding outer ripples are the effects on family and friends. These effects can even be generational. We now know that our genes have "memory" and that these traumas can be passed to our offspring.

An Internet search will show that there are few discussions on these so-called "secondary victims" of rape. Virtually all of these studies focus on the effect of the attack on the male partner of a female rape survivor. Only one study, which is available at the National Library of Medicine, from several pages of Internet search results even tried to examine the impacts on family members and friends of rape survivors. This publication determined that the interviewed friends and family found that their relationship with the survivor was often affected and that the people closest to the survivor had problems supporting them after the attack. It was also shown that some of these family and friends, despite not experiencing the attack, still suffered from PTSD symptoms.

There are resources for counseling for such secondary victims, or shall we also call them survivors? One such resource is Maryland Coalition Against Sexual Assault. These counselling services acknowledge that the individual, male or female, who experienced the physical assault is not the only person who suffers short- and long-term psychological effects.

And so, as I look back at this event and what happened after, it is with a compassion I admit I did not feel at the time that I consider the effects of the events of that night on the "secondary victims" in my life. At the time of these events, I was filled with rage and despair. I was angry at everyone, and filled with self-loathing and shame for an act that I couldn't help but think I had brought onto myself. I could barely process my own feelings, much less register that others in my life would be struggling with their own effort to cope.

My parents met me at the hospital, where I spent the rest of the night being poked and prodded, having instruments inserted in intimate places, and having my experiences and very body laid bare for an audience of strangers. I was finally released around lunchtime the next day.

My parents wanted me to eat. Isn't that what all parents want for a child they feel is injured and needs "sustenance?" After all, we call it "comfort food" for a reason, and I think that's what they hoped to accomplish. So off we went to a restaurant, as if we were greeting a normal day and not the one after their daughter was sexually assaulted and humiliated. I had no desire to go out to eat. I hadn't showered since the assault. I was dirty, greasy-haired, and just did not want to be around people. My mother did not know what else to do. When you're upset, you eat. Looking back, I know my parents were in pain. But I had to process my own pain before I could look at theirs.

I know I lashed out at my mom before going into the restaurant and was pretty sullen during. To this day, I'm surprised that I can eat Chinese food at all, though I still forego the General Tso's Chicken. It makes me ill to think of it.

After filling up on noodles and lo mein, my parents took me back to my apartment. I don't remember how long they stayed, but I finally was able to take a shower and wash the previous night off of me. I both wanted my parents to leave and wanted them to stay at the same time. If they stayed, what would we talk about? A normal conversation didn't feel right, but I couldn't talk to them about what had happened. As I stated previously, my parents were very conservative. How could I explain to them how the previous night had happened?

I was assigned a counselor in the emergency room, but no one even thought about suggesting one for my parents or my sisters, who were back at home. So Mom found therapy where she could. She told people in my church what had happened, along with my piano teacher, and several other people close to the family. I was infuriated and mortified. I already felt like people were treating me differently.

In fact, almost everyone who knew *was* treating me differently. I had suddenly become something simultaneously fragile and unclean. I felt like a dead mouse that one finds behind the refrigerator. It's rather tragic, but one just wants it far away from them as quickly as possible without any pieces of the carcass coming detached.

Now *everyone* in my life would know what had happened because my mother needed to tell someone, and that *someone* became everyone she knew. It was like being labeled with a scarlet letter, only this one was an *R* in suburban Virginia instead of an *A* in Puritan New England.

Mom also leaned heavily on my three younger sisters for emotional support, angering them and pushing them away. She didn't know what else to do at the time, but involving them in the situation wasn't helpful. It affected my relationship with my youngest sister in a profound way that we're only just starting to heal now, almost twenty years later.

My parents' generation ushered in a distrust and distaste for the mental health profession. Therapy was something reserved for people who were "disturbed" mentally, not for someone who needed to vent their anger, frustration, and sorrow over an event that hadn't even happened to them. And those disturbed people were typically incarcerated in places that would horrify us today. Electrodes, straight-jackets, and padded rooms were just the tip of the iceberg in those places, so I know why therapy wasn't something my mother considered. And my dad doesn't really like talking about his emotions, so that was a firm "no" for him as well.

These details are not simply incidental for the person who will be sexually assaulted in the next sixty-eight seconds (RAINN). They will endure the physical assault, then myriad consequences of that assault. Their family will also endure the consequences. At the time, I was so overwhelmed in my own emotional and psychological response to the assault, I could have little compassion for what others were feeling. Looking back, I know that my family did the best they could to support me and to understand what I was going through. I know that I didn't make it easy, but at the risk of sounding crass and cruel, *it wasn't about them.* I had to heal myself.

Then there was the toll the assault took on my friendships. I didn't advertise my attack, but my friend, Geoff, my "outcry witness," had told our tight-knit (at least until that time) group of friends, and pretty soon, my entire life was painted by this event.

My friends turned out to not be *real* friends, except for two who stood by me, "Simon" and "Nichelle." Simon accompanied me to my police interviews and was there when an officer informed me that the man that had assaulted me was married. I didn't think I could be more devastated at the time, but this was the one piece of information that ended up being key to obtaining justice. Simon was my rock. He encouraged me to vent, curse, rant, and rave. All through the ordeal, he remained loyal and so sweet. I was never able to cry about it around him, though. One night, as tears threatened to erupt like waters that could no longer be contained by a dam, I could tell how much my pain bothered him. He leaned in and kissed me on the forehead. No man other than my husband, not even my dad, I think, has ever done that. It touched me so deeply. Here, ironically, I had found that person who saw the specialness in me.

But ultimately, that relationship fell apart, too. He'd seen me at my worst, my weakest, slithering into my own self-loathing. Simon was also forever associated with the rape. I couldn't let it go.

Nichelle was a good friend, and though we never talked about the assault, she never changed in her friendship for me. I was the one, years later, who slowly drifted away. She remained the only string linked to that time period, and I had grown a great deal in the five years since I'd graduated from college. Unfortunately, as a result, I distanced myself from her unknowingly. I still love her with all my heart and feel bad that I disappeared on her. Simultaneously, it was too agonizing to keep that tie.

My other friends just got weird. One male asked why I didn't fight the guy off. Another male belligerently insisted I should have "poked his eyes out" and "kneed him in the groin," implying that I was somehow less of a woman for not making him pay. Yet another friend, female, wanted to go to court with me, and when I told her that not even my family was going to be in court with me because I didn't want anyone to hear the intimate details of what had happened, she stopped talking to me and even took her dislike out on Nichelle (a mutual friend) for maintaining her friendship with me. This behavior was incredibly bizarre and insensitive. Her reaction implied voyeuristic desire to hear the story, and made me cringe inside. What friend wants to hear details of a forcible sexual encounter about someone they care about? And why would you be upset about something your friend wanted you to do for them?

Why would a rape survivor want anyone to hear the details of her life spread out like butter on toast?

Regardless of what we might like to think, it's always the woman who is on trial. Was she promiscuous? *She wanted sex!* Was she scantily dressed? *She asked for it!* And on and on. Why can't a woman enjoy sex without it being thought that she wants to be raped, violated? It's been difficult for me to enjoy sex even with my husband, sometimes. If he gets too passionate, my own arousal can turn into dread or apprehension. I have flashbacks… even to this day. I know he loves me. I know he would never hurt me, never force me, yet the fear is there that our lovemaking will become non-consensual aggression. I've cried during sex with my husband. I can't imagine what that does to him. I know he wants to understand. But how can he? How can any straight male, unless they've been penetrated against their will?

The worst reaction I experienced came from a female friend whom I really looked up to. "Katie," a mother returning to finish her college degree and ten years older than me, yelled at me for calling Geoff as my outcry witness, berating me for not understanding that he was not emotionally cognizant enough to even process what had happened, much less help me with it. She then audaciously spat that she didn't believe I had been raped because "women can't be raped when they're wearing jeans." Flabbergasted, I explained that a woman can be raped at any time that she doesn't offer consent. It doesn't matter whether she's already in the throes of passion, initially whispering words of lust, and is completely unclothed. She disagreed. I also informed Katie that I was wearing a skirt; therefore, her argument was moot.

I learned later that Katie had been assaulted by a relative when she was a teenager. With that knowledge and the understanding that I gained during my counseling after the assault, I realized that she perfected this skewed inner voice to rationalize what had happened to her. Though I felt a deep compassion for Katie, our friendship (if you can call it that, knowing all this) buckled. I never saw Katie after graduation. We did exchange one email when I emailed the group to update them on my status after graduation and letting them all know that I was doing well after the hearing. She, once again, berated me for mentioning the rape. We didn't communicate thereafter. Nor did I communicate with any of the rest of the group, except for Nichelle.

You would have expected the women in my life at the time to be my advocates, to be the people telling me how strong I was to take this to court and how it wasn't my fault. Instead, they were the ones who made me feel even worse about what happened. They made me feel unworthy of support, after I'd already been made to feel unworthy of true love and affection from a man. I withdrew into myself then. I seldom went out anymore, and then had an ill-advised relationship with a guy who was not worthy of me (I was slumming). When he skipped town on a bunch of debts and speeding tickets he'd accrued, I started online dating on AOL's dating service and set a couple of in-person first dates. The thought of a negative encounter freaked me out so much that I could never follow through. Seven years later, I found the courage to date again and met and dated the wonderful man who became my husband.

I have an amazing appreciation for the women who have made the #MeToo movement such a phenomenon. I know that they, too, have probably experienced belittling or denial of their assaults because their female friends possess a need to rationalize their own assault or the fear that it might happen to them. One in three women is sexually assaulted in their lifetime, but the majority of those women don't come forward and do not press charges. I understand this, and I feel a deep sadness that part of the reason is that women morph into the biggest critics of other women when it comes to sexual assault. It's worth stating that two other women who are very close to me were raped. They will tell their stories one day, but we have to fix this.

Yes, rare women outright lie about sexual assault, which is a disgrace. I don't know what motivates them to do this, as no one craves this kind of misguided attention unless they are mentally ill. No one wants the questions, the looks, the patently weird treatment. We consider ourselves a sexually enlightened culture in the US, but we are far from it. Despite years of excessive research, exposure to the topic, and even mega-popular shows like *Law and Order: Special Victims Unit* and *CSI*, we still can't help the sneaking suspicion that women have done something to ask for their assault. We don't want to feel the gravity of the truth, the prevalence, so much so that we shun survivors. We also know now that rape has nothing to do with sex (that's right: NOTHING TO DO WITH SEX), but since it is a *sexual act*, we make it dirty in a way that only sexual assault can be made dirty.

Rape directly correlates to power, the ultimate violation of a human body.

Sex is about trust and vulnerability, especially for a woman. Consider the nature of the (heterosexual) sex act for a woman. Note that I'm not saying a woman cannot be raped by another woman but am acknowledging that the vast majority of rapists are male, even if they are raping other males. A man penetrates a woman. That penetration can be vaginal, anal, or oral. During consensual sex, consenting to this penetration is the ultimate act of trust a woman can show for her partner. She is showing true vulnerability to him at that time. He can, at any time, become rough or violent during the act. She cannot know this when she engages into the act with him.

When a man forcibly penetrates a woman, regardless of the type of penetration, he is exploiting this vulnerability and he is hurting a woman in the deepest way he can. I am not necessarily talking about the physical scars, although those can be painful and permanent. I am talking about the emotional scars—the physical dominance of a woman's body, the ownership that her rapist has while he is penetrating her. Her body is invaded. This is why, although I believe that a woman can take sexual advantage of a man, she cannot rape him in the same way that a man can rape a woman (or another man, as the penetration aspect is the same and has the same reason: domination).

Because only women can understand what it is like for a woman to be raped, I am shocked and appalled when women don't support each other during cases of rape accusation. Women must band together on this issue just like women should band together to help with discrimination in the workplace. Women need to advocate for each other. We should be in each other's back corners, not look at each other as "competition." We should show solidarity for unfair treatment of other women. I hope that the #MeToo movement really cements this solidarity, and that this solidarity carries over to the workplace.

Women can view other women in the workplace as competition due to the limited number of women. Unfortunately, when diversity and inclusion are not used properly (i.e., managers are told they need to promote a certain number of minorities), it only fosters this sense of competition. Women know that the one "token" supervision spot that the company wants to fill with a female can't be filled by the entirety of the 7 percent of women in the work group. When diversity and inclusion actually necessitate judging people by their skill set regardless of their appearance, gender, or ethnicity instead of promoting certain people to meet quotas, then women tend to advocate for each other in the workplace. Women advocating for women is important. The STEM community of industries will not change without that advocation.

SODOMY AND ADULTERY

"Justice and power must be brought together, so that whatever is just may be powerful, and whatever is powerful may be just."

—BLAISE PASCAL

I didn't tell the police the whole truth, as I said before, because I didn't want them to think less of me. I didn't tell them, for example, that I was the one who took him to the bedroom. It didn't occur to me to explain why I took him there; that I was afraid, that I was worried he was going to rape me in the living room and my roommates would walk in on us, that I was afraid he was going to kill me if I didn't cooperate—it only occurred to me that piece of information would make it look "consensual." The whole truth didn't come out until the hearing.

The hearing was so painful. It was a preliminary hearing to determine if a crime had been committed. I firmly believed in the oath I was taking, and I told the truth, the whole truth… nothing but the truth. So, help me God. I cried in spite of thinking I couldn't cry anymore. When I used the word, "raped," as in "He raped me," an objection was raised. I was told to rephrase. I had to say, "He penetrated my vagina with his penis." That was so much worse. It makes me cringe thinking of it now.

As I alluded to previously, the fact that my rapist was married was the only component that ended up delivering any form of "justice." He was charged with *sodomy and adultery*, crimes to this day in the state of Virginia. Adultery, for having sex with another person outside of his marriage, and sodomy, encompassing oral and anal sex. He was not charged with rape. But at least he was charged with something. A victory.

I don't remember if there was a trial. Again, you'd think these things would be seared into your brain in an almost physical way, but they aren't. Memory is a fickle thing, with the brain constantly editing memories as they are revisited. I do remember talking to the district attorney on the phone and telling him I wasn't interested in testifying at trial. In truth, I simply didn't think I had the strength to see him again, to literally *face him* again and say all those things in court, knowing at best, he was facing a misdemeanor. I haven't looked up the court proceedings to see whether he pled out, but I expect he did, since charges were pressed. In the end, he probably only faced a fine. I don't know what, if anything, he was ultimately found legally *guilty* of, nor do I think it would be helpful for my healing to find out.

I had the courage only very recently to Google my rapist. You see, I do remember his name. That *was* captured and retained by my memory cells. I will not provide it here. This is not about "outing" my rapist (and there would likely be legal repercussions for me— how messed up is that?—if I stated his name publicly).

I was proud of myself, as I typed the name in, hit "enter," and saw his image on the screen (part of his profile for a popular job search app), that it didn't evoke the visceral feeling that I experienced one day after the trial when I saw him on the same university bus that I was riding to class. That day, I got off at the next stop and walked home, going straight to bed. Classes weren't important to me that day. All that was important was getting away from him. However, the fact that I barely reacted at all, seeing his face on a computer screen twenty-two years later, demonstrated that he no longer has power over me (to my immense relief).

As my readers may have guessed, given that I found his picture associated with a job services profile, my rapist has gone on to have a successful career. It doesn't seem to have been stellar, but he became a professor at the university we were both attending at the time of my attack, and he is an assistant professor at another major university now. After determining this, I promptly blocked his profile. Knowing he could have looked me up any time over the past decade or so that I have maintained a profile on the same site gave me a shiver down my spine. How easy it has become to find people now, and how hard to hide from our past.

Seeing his picture and his success might almost make one doubt that anything happened at all. Perhaps I just imagined it. I searched the web for any indication that his name was publicly associated with my rape. My efforts were rewarded with one small excerpt, a transcript from a local news service. My name is not mentioned; his is. This five-sentence transcript, probably from the morning news, states that an exchange student at the university we both attended was arrested and charged with raping and sodomizing a woman he met in an Internet chat room. It provides his age and mine, making me wonder what our respective ages have to do with the act of rape. It reaffirms, in a statement of brutal simplicity, my vague intuition that he raped me multiple times and finishes by stating that he was held without bond. This is my legacy.

He went on to have a successful career, even with this information out there for anyone to find. The world is kind to men, even in the darkest aspects of our society. We live in a society of short memories, particularly for those who are educated and (yes, I'm going to say it) privileged. How many sports stars and celebrities have been accused of beating their partner, of assaulting and raping women? We eat it up when it's in the press, feasting on every lurid detail. We talk about what an awful person they are to fight dogs or punch a woman in the face and drag her by the hair on camera. Then the next big thing comes along, and we forget.

The detective who was my case officer during the whole ordeal was a very nice man. I remember his last name, an ironic reminder echoed in the very title of this book. I think he understood my motivations. As he said later, he was "disappointed" that I didn't feel comfortable telling him the whole truth. He knew that "something really bad" happened to me and was upset that I hadn't disclosed the truth early on, so the discrepancies made me look like a liar on the stand. I had the impression that the officer faced these types of events before. But I think he also knew that the likelihood of getting any better result from the hearing was slim because it was a date rape. He was satisfied with the sodomy and adultery charge.

The silver lining is that my rapist's name is in the system. His DNA is in the system. In talking over the results of the hearing with my case officer, he admitted his opinion that the methodology used by my rapist was probably one he had used before, relying on the fact that his victim would be ashamed to come forward. He told me that date rape was incredibly common for this very reason: the rapist knew that shame, regret, and self-blame would be parlayed into buyer's remorse, even if the word "no" was used. Who's to say he didn't do it again? His career success is not predicated on his having "learned his lesson."

Consent is such a powerful concept, and one that I still don't think society has a real grasp of. Think about a child (whether male or female doesn't matter) who says "no" to hugging a family member. What do we typically do? We cajole the child into hugging their aunt, uncle, grandfather, or cousin whether they really want to or not. We don't acknowledge their right to consent to the simple act of hugging someone. And if the parent stands in support of their child, and says "No, they don't have to hug you. Let them alone," then we're met with words like "It's just a hug," or "I'm his grandmother. I'm entitled to hug my grandchild," or "They're a child. It's not up to them to decide. I'm the adult."

We override the consent of our children because we don't consider them to have valid feelings. This is why it's so easy to claim that a child is "making up" their own sexual assault. Children don't make up things like that. They don't have a frame of reference for those behaviors. An adult is viewed as a protector, especially an adult who is close to the child such as a family member or parent.

It wasn't so long ago that women weren't considered to have valid feelings, either. I still think this feeling pervades our society. It's well-known that women are treated differently by doctors than men and often don't receive the proper medical treatment because they are considered "hysterical" and "overly emotional." This leads to many women being told it's "all in their head."

While I hope that my rapist did not assault any other women, I am glad I am responsible for his DNA being taken and for charges being brought so that another woman might receive full justice. That said, I can't say for sure if I would make the same decision if I had it all to do over again. If I was able to do it with the knowledge and maturity I have now, I'd tell the entire truth up front and take the punches as they came. But without the knowledge and maturity I have now, I don't know. I wish I could say I'd be courageous regardless of the outcome. I'm unsure. I hope my readers don't judge me too harshly for that. If you do, though, that is your right, and I'm okay with that. I'm at peace with my decisions and the outcome. Maybe that's all one can hope for: peace.

I am legally a survivor of "sodomy and adultery." The word "survivor" is still not one I have grown friendly with. In fact, it still leaves a rancid taste in my mouth. I roll it around, trying to get it into a position where it doesn't still feel like a euphemism for something else. Legally, I didn't "survive" anything. I experienced it, and it was illegal. Does that diminish my experience? In some ways, it does. But knowing that many rape cases, especially in that era, and especially in instances of date rape, didn't have that positive an outcome. Many women never report; many more, like me, can't stomach the thought of a trial after completing the initial hearing, often leading to plea deals on far lesser charges. Does that diminish their experience? I don't think so, and I hope you don't either.

CHAPTER 2

SERVICE

HIGHLY ENRICHED WOMAN

"My own brain is to me the most unaccountable of machinery—always buzzing, humming, soaring roaring diving, and then buried in mud. And why? What's this passion for?"

—VIRGINIA WOOLF

WRITING FOR *FORBES*, Rick Miller asks, "What is power, really?" He asserts, "Power is available to everyone, no matter their position or title. Real power is *influence*, and it increases as we offer more *support* to others. Being powerful is more about giving support than getting support. Contrary to what you may have thought about power, service is the highest form of leadership. Serving others is a key to sustainable growth. And it creates the kind of influence that truly powerful people wield—the kind that resonates and uplifts."

Given the intensity of chronicles in Chapter 1, I prefer to stay in *this* category of power for a little while, so settle in! Miller also defines power as clarity, energy, impact, and confidence. It's a comfortable genre of power for many. By no means am I stating that these corridors of power are not hard to achieve or painless, though.

I am an engineer in the nuclear power sector. In brief, and for the purpose of diffusing the myth that we simply blow things up or create dangerous devices all day long, a nuclear engineer's work generally consists of writing instruction and training individuals on nuclear plant operation, performing tests and experiments on different nuclear materials, and designing safe and efficient specialized nuclear equipment for medical or reactor use. There are three main fields in the industry: thermal hydraulics (focus on heat transfer and fluid flow and is similar to what is studied in chemical and mechanical engineering), radiation detection and measurement (health physics and safety), and reactor physics (mainly work with neutron transport in a nuclear reactor).

I've been in the industry since I started my career on July 2, 2007, as an Engineer I at a company working to complete the site-specific designs for one of the advanced reactor designs. These reactors are known for their so-called "passive" safety features, meaning the plant design doesn't use a lot of pumps or valves that require electricity to power them. Instead, they focus on natural circulation or gravity, forces of nature that are always available even if the power is interrupted (which happened at Fukushima). The nuclear renaissance was in full swing. In fact, between 2007 and 2009, thirteen companies applied to the Nuclear Regulatory Commission (NRC) for construction and operating licenses to build thirty-one new nuclear power reactors in the United States.

Fast forward twelve years, and all but two of those projects were cancelled. The last one to be cancelled, on July 31, 2017, was VC Summer Units 2 and 3, the project on which my husband and I were working at that time.

As of the time of writing, the only new reactor that has been completed is Watts Bar Unit 2. Watts Bar Unit 2 was constructed under the old Part 50 rule—10 CFR 50—where first a construction and then a separate operating license were issued. A search of the NRC website yields the following information: Operating License granted 10/22/2015, Plant Design—Westinghouse Four-Loop (meaning the reactor cooling system has four separate cooling loops). The NRC website also provides the megawatt rating of the unit and the type of containment the plant has. This is only a fraction of the information available to the public on the NRC website.

Vogtle Units 3 and 4, both of the AP1000 design are currently under construction just outside Augusta, Georgia, and are slated to be the first (and only) full-scale nuclear plants built under the Part 52 process (10 CFR 52). Incidentally, the regulation—10 CFR 52—and all other parts of 10 CFR (Code of Federal Regulations) is available on the NRC website for review, as well. Vogtle Units 3 and 4 have been in the press a lot, of late, due to budget overruns and schedule delays.

There is plenty of information out there on the Vogtle 3 and 4 project, as well as the V.C. Summer Units 2 and 3 project, so I'm not going to go into those details here. I'm also not going to discuss anything that's not available to the public, so if you were hoping for a tell-all on that subject, then I must disappoint.

It's been well-publicized that both projects were over budget. The ramifications of the budget and schedule issues are also well-publicized.

As an advocate for nuclear power, seeing the V.C. Summer project cancelled was devastating for me from both a personal and professional standpoint. Seeing one project crippled and brought to its knees by budget overruns, poor planning, and out-of-touch project oversight was infuriating. But also, watching people I'd worked with for over two years disband and move their entire families to other locations was heartbreaking. These people were family, and I still miss them every day.

That project was a defining point in my career. It was the end of my participation in the nuclear renaissance (or pretty close to it, as you'll see further on), and it was the beginning of my career as an employee of a utility. While to some extent the differences between the environments in which I worked were varied, to the larger extent, my *experience* in the industry has been fairly homogenous.

I spent just over three years at my first employer working on the advanced passive reactor design after beginning my career in 2007. My company was working on what was termed the "site-specific" portion of the design and was working primarily on four projects. The "standard plant" portion of the design was being completed by the so-called "NSSS provider" (Nuclear Steam Supply system, referred to as "N triple S"), which, in the nuclear parlance, is the acronym given to the reactor design itself. This part of the design is proprietary and specific to a certain company. The major NSSS players still in business, some of whose names you might have heard, are companies such as Westinghouse, Mitsubishi, GE Hitachi, and B&W. You can research the various reactor designs on the NRC website. If you hear that a design is a "Westinghouse three-loop" design, that means that Westinghouse is the "NSSS supplier" and the design has a three-loop reactor coolant system. The NRC website (nrc.gov) is a great reference for the different plant designs.

When I started out on my first advanced reactor design, the AP1000, I was working on the standard design for the wastewater system, the collection and treatment system for the effluent water in the plant. My first major calculation was to determine a standard design for the wastewater retention basin (WWRB). Note the nuclear industry *loves* its acronyms. I was then moved over to another project to work on the circulating water system design. As part of those duties, I performed sizing calculations for the system including the pump horsepower and cooling tower heat removal requirements. I also handled the subcontract for the natural draft cooling towers and wrote purchase specifications for various pieces of equipment. I worked on three "subsystems" for the circulating water system—the cooling tower, the chemical treatment, and the overall closed-cooling portion of the system.

These details and scope of explicit professional experience serve as the backdrop for following the tale concerning power.

Shortly after I started my duties on the circulating water system, one of the four projects my company was working on was put on hold (a move that, in hindsight, was ominous and presaged the overall future of the project). My project absorbed some of the team members from this "on-hold" project, and to accomplish that absorption, the circulating water system was removed from my ownership and was assigned to a much more senior male engineer (I'll call him "Walt"). I was then reassigned to "assist" this engineer and the other much more senior male engineer ("Jack"), who had the raw water system (the system that provided water from the river to the plant for makeup to the circulating water system, via the basins on the cooling towers). I want to emphasize that when stating "much more senior," I am referring both to experience *and* age, an important feature in this book exploring power and fragility.

In what I would think was a natural turn of thought, I assumed this reassignment was both about absorbing these other employees into the Vogtle team *and* a commentary on my performance as a system engineer. I say this was "natural" because as assistant to these two men, I, in essence, did all the work (wrote the calculations, system descriptions, and specifications) for them to review as "experts." So, I did all the work for none of the credit. How could that be anything but a reflection of my abilities to manage the system on my own without "direction?"

One day, I approached the project engineer and asked him rather bluntly, "Can you please tell me what I was doing wrong that made the project reassign me like this?"

To his credit, he looked very sheepish. "Stan" was a good man, and I never encountered any hint of sexism from him. Yes, you can usually spot or sense it a mile away as a professional woman in a male-dominated industry. With that, Stan did adjust and scratch his crotch in my presence a bit more than I was comfortable with, but I would need to condemn all men for that behavior if I were being completely truthful.

Stan insisted that the decision had not been his; it had been my supervisor's. So, let's talk about my supervisor at that time. We'll call him "Nar." Nar seemed to have an issue with appropriateness when it came to dealing with women. By this, I don't mean to say he was sexually inappropriate. Far from it. He was about as austere as you can be. What I mean is that he didn't seem to possess an appreciation for women as equals. As evidence in my case, I cite the time that he asked a female friend of mine (also an engineer), who had just had a baby three months before, when her baby was due. Sure, that could just be a *faux pas*, an instance of a man sticking his foot squarely into his mouth, and I might give him a pass if that were the only instance of apparent sexism.

Then there's the time when he, the two senior male engineers whom I was assisting, Walt and Jack, and I were in a meeting discussing the schedule for designing the circulating water and raw water systems. I had just redone the schedule for circulating water and was quite proud of it. It had garnered numerous compliments from project management, which was feedback I definitely needed at that time in my career when I was still developing my confidence. As we were reviewing the schedules, with the aim of making the raw water schedule similar to the circulating water schedule (another compliment from the two senior engineers), I made a suggestion starting with, "In my opinion… " Nar responded,

"Well, your opinion no longer matters."

That's the first time I cried at work. Luckily not in that meeting, but later. I held it together through that statement, through the pitying looks from the two male engineers, who were markedly uncomfortable, but not enough to actually *say* anything or rally to my defense, and through the rest of the meeting. Then I escaped to the restroom (How many women have?) and opened my trunk of tears.

Yes, my feelings were hurt. How would they not be? To be put down, and publicly, in that manner is hurtful. But mostly, I was pissed. I was furious that I had spent a massive amount of effort to be told my opinion "didn't matter." The following day was when

I confronted Stan. I'd already surmised the conversation with Nar wouldn't go well regarding my reassignment.

Stan reaffirmed what I'd already known with his side of the reassignment story. "I told Nar it was a bad idea and that you'd see it as a commentary on the quality of your work, which, by the way, is exemplary. I want you to know that. But Nar isn't great with women. I think there are some cultural issues there. I've tried to explain this to him, but it doesn't seem to register."

I recall that incident with Nar as my first real experience with sexism in my career. I wish I could say it was my last. The end result was that I got the circulating water system back and I'm proud to say that when I finally left that company, it took three engineers to replace me: one to manage the overall system, one to manage the cooling tower, and one to manage the chemical treatment subsystem.

I left my first job because of what I perceived to be a delayed promotion. Other engineers (all of whom were male) had been promoted after two years at the company. I was constantly given the feedback that I was doing the work of an Engineer III or even an Engineer IV based on what the expectations were at this company for their engineers. And yet, no promotion was forthcoming. So, I started looking for another opportunity in the area.

At my next company, I was the sole person responsible for the cooling tower subcontract for a project whose aim was to build a single unit at a site in Virginia that was already home to two existing units. At that time, this project was pursuing another advanced passive reactor design, the Mitsubishi-designed US-APWR. The cooling tower design was extremely unique, a *hybrid, plume-abated natural draft tower*, as they are called. It was a great opportunity. Plus, it had the benefit of frequent trips back home to Central Virginia, since I would have to visit the construction site every once in a while.

While I was with my second company, Gene proposed to me,

and bursting with happiness, I couldn't say (shout), "yes" quickly enough. Gene was actually so excited about proposing that night that he left the house, where we were living together at the time, without his wallet. I had to pay for dinner, and he really thought he'd ruined the night. He didn't propose at the restaurant, so I figured he'd given up on proposing that night and would do it another time. But instead, as soon as he verified his wallet was on the nightstand, he dropped to one knee and popped the question. It was so cute and his eagerness so endearing, that of course I had to say "yes."

During this time, my confidence as an engineer increased exponentially. I enjoyed my time at this company, and it was fairly benign. I worked closely with Mitsubishi engineers (who called me "Karle-san," which I will always think of fondly), and learned a lot about the Japanese culture, as a result. I likely would have stayed on at this company longer, had Gene not been offered an excellent position (an offer we couldn't refuse) at what we call an AE (architect/engineer) firm located in Maryland. He turned them down at first, insisting that he would not move unless they could also find a position for me. What a considerate, exceptional partner to risk his career trajectory like that for me. Fortunately, after some negotiation, we were able to make it work and we relocated to Maryland in August 2011.

That's how I found myself on yet another new project, this time designing the extraction steam system for one of the few small modular reactor (SMR) designs being pursued at that time. The U.S. Department of Energy defines SMRs as reactor designs with a nominal output of <300 MWe. The term "modular," in the context of an SMR, refers to a single reactor module that can be grouped with other reactor modules to form a larger nuclear power plant, sized according to demand. Although the utility-scale advanced reactors currently under construction incorporate factory-fabricated modular components into their designs, a substantial amount of field work is still required to assemble these modules into an operational nuclear power plant. SMRs, on the other hand, are envisioned to require limited on-site preparation, and—other than loading the nuclear fuel—be ready to operate when they arrive from the factory. My role on this project was relatively powerful, needless to say.

During my tenure at my third employer, Gene and I got married. I also accomplished a monumental goal: obtaining my Professional Engineer license. It was a good time in my personal and professional life. I was honored after working for on the project for two years to be given the opportunity to do a stint in licensing, which meant that the responsibility of writing "design certification document" chapters for the license that was to be submitted to the Nuclear Regulatory Commission (NRC). This would have been one of the first SMRs to apply for NRC licensing, so I was excited to, once again, be at the forefront of the nuclear renaissance.

The first reactor of this design was initially going to be placed at a site in Tennessee. That never came to fruition, unfortunately. In what would be a foreshadowing of the end of the V. C. Summer project that I worked on years later, the project's costs started to escalate, and it was cancelled before it even took off. After just under three years on the SMR project, it was time to knock on doors for work unless I relocated to one of the few projects that had a large budget for staff at the time, located in Washington State. Unfortunately, they didn't have plans to send Gene out there, as well. I had no desire to move across the country by myself, without my husband of a little over a year. It would also have been difficult to be that far away from my family, who are primarily located in Central Virginia. So, I decided to take a job with another AE firm, one with an impressive 250-year history, in the Atlanta area in July of 2014. I figured if I had to work in a different state, I could at least stay on the same coast as my husband and family.

I spent nine months in Georgia with this company. For part of that time, Gene was still in Maryland, working with my previous employer, where he still had a job since his skill set was needed. I don't think he realized how much it rankled that they wanted to keep him, but were willing to send me to the Pacific Northwest. In fact, it was his desirability as an employee that led to me taking the job in the Atlanta area, even though I knew I'd be separated from Gene. We went on a joint interview at an AE firm in Delaware. My interview was going fairly well, but as soon as they realized who I was married to (you see, he'd worked for this AE firm before and was very well-respected) I became a secondary concern. Once again, an employer was willing to give us a package deal just to get my husband. As flattering as that might seem (she says in a very sarcastic tone), I thought I was far enough along in my career to be desired for my own talents and skills.

While Gene was still in Maryland, I saw him once a month, when he would either fly down or drive. That situation was untenable. He tried several times to snatch up a position with my employer in Georgia, but for some reason, they just weren't interested, which was a rather interesting turn of events and one neither of us expected. Gene decided to apply at V. C. Summer with the current constructor, who had purchased the nuclear arm of the company I started my career within the period during which we were both in Maryland. He was able to get a job there and for the next six months or so, Gene would drive down to Atlanta Thursday nights, stay until Sunday night, and drive back to South Carolina to be at work the next morning. Luckily Thanksgiving and Christmas weeks that year we got to spend together, but it was a miserable existence.

After eight months, I was done, and I applied at V. C. Summer, myself. I started in March of 2015. Essentially, I started and ended the Architect Engineer portion of my career with the same company because by this time, the nuclear arm of my first company had been bought by yet another company. I had come full circle. A fitting end to the first decade of my career.

POWER(FUL) SCHOOL

"We want the education by which character is formed,
strength of mind is increased, the intellect is expanded,
and by which one can stand on one's own feet."

—Swami Vivekananda

NUCLEAR POWER SCHOOL is the popular moniker given to the navy's nuclear reactor training program. A part of the Naval Nuclear Power Training Command, this school is responsible for training navy personnel to use the reactors that power the many nuclear warships, air-craft carriers, and submarines used by the U.S. Navy. The World Nuclear Association estimates there were 108 nuclear-powered vessels in the U.S. fleet in 2019. The navy's nuclear program started in the 1950s. The first female candidates graduated nuclear power school in 2011. For sixty years, the nuclear navy was relegated only to men. But that doesn't mean that women haven't made it into the so-called civilian nuclear industry. Some, like myself, have come to it by rather unusual, but equally power-ful, means.

When I started my career in 2007, I had freshly earned a mas-ter's degree in physics and completed the first two years of a Ph.D. in medical physics. I left the Ph.D. program when my advisor, "Dr. Karl," left his professorship to pursue research in the private sector. That is, he left to make more money! I can't blame him. The world of academia is brutal. You work your ass off for a pittance salary (although medical physics does pay more than most areas of study) and live in a world of "publish or die." I was definitely bitter at the time, but I no longer begrudge Dr. Karl the better opportunity he saw for himself. In fact, armed with the more mature perspective I have now, I applaud his choice.

My master's degree focused on surface science, but I took a lot of classes in medical physics. I really enjoyed medical physics, enough to want to pursue a Ph.D. in the subject. Had I stayed in the program after Dr. Karl left, I would have been one of the first few that the program had graduated, and one of only two women in the program at that time. The research I was working on with Dr. Karl was groundbreaking at the time. We were trying to package an MRI contrast agent and a PET imaging radio-nuclide into some type of molecular cage so that they could be delivered in the same intra-venous (IV) solution prior to imaging.

MRI, which stands for magnetic resonance imaging, operates using the physics of magnetism that exists in every element in nature. In some elements, the magnetic field is very weak, so you need a strong magnet to incite the magnetic poles in the element to align. That's what MRI does to the human body. Talk about power! The human body is composed mostly of water, but each body tissue contains a different water composition (muscle is different than fat, is different than brain tissue, etc.). And cancerous tumors have a different water composition than all of these body tissues. MRI exploits this characteristic to create images.

This is quite profound. Picture a flat plane, like a piece of paper. Then picture a vector perpendicular to that flat plane, like an arrow with its base stuck to the paper and the arrow sticking straight up from the paper. The flat plane is the X, Y plane and the arrow is the Z direction. Now, imagine a very strong rotating magnetic field, a giant electromagnet (that's the *whomp, whomp* you hear from the MRI) inciting a sympathetic magnetic field in the fluids in your body. It is basically so strong that it causes all of the poles to align to the Z axis. Then, as the magnetic field wanes, the poles in the tissues of your body begin to "fall" back into the X, Y plane. They all do this at a different rate. And this rate is what the MRI machine is capturing as an image. This creates the most detailed imaging of any of the modalities without the use of contrast agents.

Contrast agents are solutions of various substances (some radioactive; some not), depending on the imaging modality, that are preferentially absorbed by certain tissues to further enhance structures in the body. To enhance MRI, a contrast agent that is highly magnetizable is used. Gadolinium is probably the most common MRI contrast agent. It is preferentially taken up by the tumor and allows MRI to provide even better details on the boundaries of a tumor. In a hypothetical dual MRI/PET imaging agent, gadolinium would likely be the first choice for the MRI contrast agent since it is relatively inexpensive and has a sufficient history of reliable and safe imaging.

PET is positron emission tomography, which examines the metabolism of body tissues, but can also be used to analyze blood flow, regional chemical composition, and absorption. PET uses radioactive substances to create images instead of using a magnetic field. Each tissue in the body has a different metabolic rate. PET relies on a contrast agent to help to "highlight" the metabolic differences between a cancer tumor (cells divide rapidly, so it's *highly* metabolic) and normal tissue. F-18 is very good at binding to the sugar receptors, which is why it is one of the most common radionuclides used for PET imaging. F-18 is readily available due to its routine use in PET imaging, so it could be paired with gadolinium. In fact, many studies have used both of these modalities with gadolinium contrast MRIs and F-18 PET imaging to localize tumors.

Now, imagine if you could put both of those agents in the same package. You would need a material that was relatively inert. Something that wasn't magnetic and wouldn't interfere with the MRI image and something non-radioactive that wouldn't skew the

PET image. Carbon is an inert substance, so what if you could put the gadolinium and the F-18 inside some type of carbon cage? The astute reader is probably ahead of me now. Buckyballs (*Buckminster fullerenes*), could be used in such a hypothetical imaging agent. Their structure provides a sort of cage that one can insert various molecules into. This would allow MRI, which gives the cleanest demarcations of the edges of the tumor, to be combined with PET imaging, which gives the best indication of how aggressive the tumor is, based on its glucose metabolism, to assist in diagnosing and locating the tumors. Now, this is all hypothetical, of course, but we were working to make something like this a reality. We performed some initial studies in rats, which, I admit, bothered me a great deal, as I'd had them as pets before. But it would have been a fantastic project to carry through to completion and to have my name on a published paper.

When Dr. Karl left, it was challenging trying to find someone to take me on as a research assistant. I had spent two years on one project, and no one else wanted to invest the time to catch me up so that I could still graduate on the original schedule. If I had possessed the confidence then that a fourteen-year career has afforded me, I might have pushed harder to stay. At the time, I had just passed the Ph.D. qualifying exams, leading me to an offer for a position with the renowned Dr. Karen Kurdziel, MD (finally a real name), now a board-certified nuclear medicine physician, writing image-manipulation software, which would have been epic had I felt capable as a programmer.

Are you getting the picture of power and fragility in this chapter? Even loaded with a hearty education and exclusive opportunities, lack of confidence is a bitch. You can feel quite capable on one side of the coin and completely powerless and ill-equipped on the other. Which side shines more? Usually, the one of weakness because it tends to dictate decision making. My earlier self-esteem issues and trauma could not be degreed over.

Having decided to take a leave of absence from the Ph.D. program at VCU, I took my first job in the nuclear industry, working on the first new nuclear development in thirty years. I started my career as a shy, extremely introverted young engineer. As the first three years of my career progressed, though, I rapidly gained confidence in my abilities, both technically and in presence. Not only did I discover that I was skillful at the analysis required by my job (primarily flow modeling to determine pump sizing, verify pipe sizing, and analyze water hammer impacts to the various fluid systems we were responsible for designing); I was also skilled at writing the technical documents supporting that analysis and presenting supporting technical discussions to my management and to our customers. That's not to say that my time here was without issue, as I have already alluded to. The one thing that I am incredibly grateful to my first company for is meeting my husband, Gene, a source of great support and love.

Fortunately, at my first company, there were more women in the engineering group than would typically be in an engineering firm. This wasn't through any Affirmative Action or Diversity Hiring initiative, it was just that they were looking for young (cheap) engineers to do the work in a cost-effective manner. I was surrounded by women, and we became fast friends. Almost all of the women were mid-twenties in age, while the men in the office were either mid-twenties or late forties/early fifties. The generation gap was quite noticeable in the male contingent, but not as much in the female contingent because the last time they built nuclear plants, women were even fewer and farther between as engineers than they are today.

After a series of events that were not corrected by management (a trend I would continue to experience when I returned to the same management structure in South Carolina later in my career), I decided to leave the company, while staying local, and I took a position with a company also working on a first-of-a-kind nuclear power plant design, while Gene stayed with Shaw. My position at my second employer was similar to that with the first, doing site-specific system design for a new nuclear power plant.. This was also the one opportunity my husband and I have had so far in our careers since we've been together to stay in the same city, but work for different companies. As you've probably noticed so far, when both spouses work in the same industry (Gene is an electrical engineer, and we both work in the nuclear power industry), it can lead to a decidedly nomadic lifestyle.

In general, my keen observation of my third employer was that it was very much a quintessential Boys Club, with all the trimmings, yet it wouldn't be the only one I found myself standing in the center of, like Dante Alighieri in Inferno, and with few female engineers.

I celebrated a decade in the new nuclear industry in July of 2017. Unfortunately, this was after the beginning of the end had started for the V.C. Summer project. In fact, not even a month after my glitzy anniversary in the industry, the V.C. Summer project was cancelled due to a slew of problems. There has been a lot of press on the topic, and there's a lot of truth to the coverage. Still, as with every industry, department and project, there is a great deal that only insiders can grasp.

Those of us on the V.C. Summer project were devastated by the cancellation. Many team members are still devastated, as evidenced by the closed social media groups that were established to communicate and share resources after the project was cancelled. I still miss that team, those people, the laughter, and the commiseration. I have not experienced another work group like that one. I truly love those people. There is power in community. There is power in shared accomplishments that are not tainted by gender, salary or title wars.

I'd been approached some time before V. C. Summer was cancelled for a position with my current employer, a nuclear power station in Central Virginia. (The name of my current employer has an eerie coincidence with events that occurred earlier in my life.) Since this position would be close to family, I was already interested and had done a web-based preliminary interview. On July 31, though, the need for another job was evident, as both Gene and I had been put on unpaid leave when the project was officially cancelled. I took a trip to the plant for an in-person interview the week after we were sent home from V.C. Summer. Then I waited.

Gene and I were both unemployed for three weeks before we were each offered a position at the Vogtle Units 3 and 4 site, which is the site of the only other AP1000 plants being constructed in the United States. During the time we'd been laid off, I'd been applying for jobs elsewhere, since Augusta, Ga. was not where we were interested in settling. We'd had plans at V. C. Summer for me to stay on as a system engineer and for my husband to retire (he is twenty years older than me). We loved Lexington, South Carolina and would very much have liked to stay there and have an extended career.

I eventually was offered a position at the power plant. After weighing the likelihood of Vogtle continuing, given what we knew at the time about V.C. Summer, the Westinghouse bankruptcy, and the project costs, we decided that I should take the job. A utility job would offer more stability and the opportunity to have a career—not the nomadic job-to-job lifestyle that we had been enjoying up to that point. So, after biding time while my background check was processed, I started my current job on October 30, 2017.

Gene stayed at Vogtle. A year passed. This was an excruciating existence for both of us. I was deeply unhappy in my new job, and the added stress of our long-distance relationship (the second we'd experienced in less than six years of marriage) pushed me to the brink. I ended up on the phone with my husband one night crying and telling him he needed to come home, even if that meant quitting. That we'd be okay financially, I just needed him home. He put in his resignation letter, and we made plans for him to come home.

At the eleventh hour, Westinghouse came back and offered, "What about a rotational schedule? Can you be here two weeks and then work from home two weeks?" Gene and I discussed it at length and decided that it was a good compromise. We wanted to buy a house in Virginia, so it gave us the financial flexibility to be able to do that with a two-to-three-year plan in which we could work towards Gene coming home. That was almost two years ago, as of this writing. Many people who work in this industry have it a lot worse, being farther apart and for longer. I know the nuclear industry isn't the only one where families are separated for long periods of time, and I keep that in perspective. But it doesn't make it easy. At times, my deepest enclave of fragility is related to isolation.

AN ENGINEER'S PAIN SCALE

*"Out of suffering have emerged the strongest souls; the
most massive characters are seared with scars."*

—KHALIL GIBRAN

FOR A FEW weeks during our spring outage, I attended the 8:00 a.m. "engineering alignment" meeting for my boss, who was on night shift. I was the youngest person in the room most mornings (except on the weekends, when other engineers would be in the meeting representing their supervision). There was one African American manager in the meetings. And I was the only female in the room.

As a funny (but not humorous) story, and an example of the unthinking attitude that some men have in the industry, go ahead and dissect a discussion held during that morning meeting. "Brad," one of the engineering supervisors who worked in the OCC (Outage Control Center) during our outages, was describing an argument held by three other men in the OCC the previous afternoon. He explained how tempers had gotten frayed due to the long hours, and things escalated more than they should have. Basically, he told us, it's natural for things like that to happen, but when they do, we should take the conversation to a private room and not air it in the middle of a room full of other people. His statement was 100% correct (things like this are normal, but how and where we have such discussions are critical), but the specific phrasing he used for the three people involved in the argument were telling on several levels. As Brad put it, "T levels got elevated."

I laughed to myself over this statement. First, I hopped up on my moral high horse and thought, *well, that's something they'd never say if women were running the job.* Secondly, I considered the demographic in the room. A majority of men over the age of fifty-five (many over sixty and pushing sixty-five or older) and me: population of one female. Lastly, I considered the complete obliviousness by Brad that such a statement might be in poor taste (even if it were funny) in a work meeting that contained only one female. But Brad tends to be oblivious. He'll make statements like "Go rub his back a little bit, make him feel better about such-and-such piece of information." I've also heard "Go blow in his ear. He'll change his mind." (Eww.) Now, if a woman said something like that, whether to a man or to another woman, how do you think that would go over?

I feel like that's the real question men should ask themselves. "How would I feel or how would it sound if a woman said this?" For instance, how would it sound if a woman said, "You'll like Dan. He's a real sweetheart."? I've heard men at my office say this about women they work with. Or, what if a woman said, "They gave me a boy. I wanted a girl. Snip it off!" as a joke about an extra electrical connection that someone asked how to wire up? My supervisor actually made that statement right in front of me.

I recently read statistics that stated that engineering demographics are (abysmally) 93% male, 83% white, with an average age of fifty. Sadly, as you can see from just one example above, my current workplace bears that out. This makes me part of the seven percent. Seven percent! How is that possible in today's era of STEM, *Lean In*, and an extremely popular female vice president? Being part of the seven percent means being a distinct minority. And if you're a minority female, the hardships are so much worse. It means your voice is muffled. Even if you complain, little is done. There are no sweeping cultural changes, no matter how much they are necessary. And, as you can probably tell from what I've shared so far, they are necessary.

In the years that I have worked, and again, I am not being specific to a company, the following things have been said in my presence:

- "Daily de-brief? I've never been a fan of briefs myself. I prefer boxers."
- "I guess your wife has to remind you to zip up your pants after you pee, too."
- "Babe."
- "Sweetheart."
- "Honey."
- "Pussy" on a work-related phone call, on two occasions.

A particular favorite occurred during a plant walkdown with two team members, both of whom were male, and one of whom was my supervisor. One team member (not my supervisor) put his finger into a small manually operated valve to see if it was open or closed, since the position wasn't readily discernable from the position of the operator. When he inserted his finger into the valve opening, he said, "It won't go all the way in; it's too big," paused for effect, and followed with "And that's what she said." *Yeah.*

I've been sent hearts and heart-eyed smiley faces by male co-workers (not my husband).

Two coworkers have alluded to spanking me. One of those was after I was married, and the man knew I was married. (You might be curious to know my husband's reaction. He wasn't as angry as I thought, and yes, hoped he'd be!) This second instance that took place after I was married was also reported to HR and to our mutual functional manager. The functional manager called me afterwards, a little too boastfully suggesting that the individual would be call-ing to apologize (implying he had something to do with this), and then urged, "But you have to remember, it's just the way he is."

During a training class in which I was the only woman, a male instructor walked us through a scenario and set it off with, "Now, I don't want you all to go running out of here screaming like little girls when I start this." At this one, I locked eyes with the instructor and quipped, "I'll do my best." Everyone laughed. He did have the grace to look a little sheepish when he responded, "Now, you know I wasn't talking about you. I was talking about these jerks cutting up behind you." Let's address the elephant in the room: To imply that someone is less strong, a "girl" is frequently attached to the reference. Last time I checked, my body is capable of creating *life*. There is nothing more powerful. Women possess much higher pain tolerance than men; there's no way men could give birth. How do you think it makes a woman feel to be considered second best in such an obvious and rather insulting fashion?

Granted, I know that the instructor didn't really *mean* anything demeaning. I know that he respects my intelligence and skill and wouldn't dream of paying me any insult. Still, it served in its own way to single me out, when I already felt like I had to work harder and be better than the men in the class to be considered on the same playing field. And, honestly, it's worse, in my opinion, to have these ingrained, unthinking phrases pelted at you than to stand toe to toe with a man who says he doesn't think women should be engineers.

Which brings me to the time when I was told females didn't make good engineers by a male engineer who was going to be reviewing one of my calculations. Suspecting there just might be some bias there, and that a review would be compromised, I addressed this concern to my supervisor. His response was to tell me that if I didn't work the issue out with the male engineer, he would force us to share a cubicle until we "got along" as if we were toddlers on the playground. When that issue eventually cycled over to HR, the supervisor retaliated against me, accusing me of absenteeism for taking two Mondays off five weeks apart, and I was moved to a different group not under his supervision.

I have been yelled at by managers, like finger-pointed-in-my-face-"just do it, damn it"-type yelling and not backed up by my supervisory chain when I complained. We all know this behavior isn't acceptable regardless of the other person's gender in a professional environment.

The topic of "strippers and prostitutes" is prevalent. During one meeting, a male co-worker showed a late-night talk show video that he claimed had an individual in it who was a dead ringer for one of the supervisors in our department. In this video, the talk show host cajoles his male producer into taking off his shirt (a harassing behavior in itself). The producer removes his shirt and is naked from the waist up for a large portion of the video. This special screening had no work-related purpose and was inappropriate. Then there was the male employee who was showing pictures on his phone of a man in a shirt that said "I'm not gay, but $20 is $20." This is what passes for (appropriate) humor among the males I have worked with.

The overarching principle at play here is *professionalism*. It's an office, a workplace, not happy hour with the workplace friends where the conversation can be relaxed, and where I can feel free to call someone out on their statements, in kind. Why is it still such a struggle for people to be respectful at work?

Here's something else to consider. Most women do not feel like they can be themselves at work, especially in the nuclear industry. In male-dominated industries, women are instructed to advocate more for themselves and to essentially have a more "male-oriented" outlook on their jobs. We're told to negotiate hard for salary or raises, to be more confident in how we present ourselves in meetings, to sit at the table.

While it may be true that women need to actively work on their confidence, many of the tasks that women are told to do at work are antithetical to the female personality archetype. The female archetype is one in which the other is always more important than the self. So, we may not advocate for ourselves the way we would for another. The male archetype is one in which the self is more important than the other. Men have no problem singing their own praises. To women, many men are braggarts. To men, many women are "too quiet," people who don't speak up and who are too passive.

When we demand that a woman be more like men to be taken seriously, I don't think we consider how that might demoralize her. The song is funny when Henry sings it in *My Fair Lady*: "Why can't a woman be more like a man?" he laments when he is trying to reason out why the object of his rant is upset at being –you got it—objectified. But we women know why Iliza is hurt and, yes, PISSED. We see men get to be themselves, but women have to put on armor to go to work every day. We have to gird ourselves to "play with the boys." Despite the changing times, no one has yet suggested in a professional setting that the men soften their approach and meet the women in the middle. I understand if they don't even meet the women halfway because there is such a huge discrepancy between the numbers of men and women in nuclear power. But to not even try to see things through the lens of a woman's viewpoint is disheartening and I dare say, rude and disrespectful.

I am an introvert by nature. I am also a modest person, who not only doesn't sing her own praises but seldom sees anything she does as being particularly exemplary—even when it is. This is borne out by research that shows that women tend to view good performance as just doing their job while men view good performance as something praiseworthy. This also plays into the fact that women are promoted for performance, while men are promoted based on their potential.

Women also have to shut down our emotions in a male-dominated workplace. Men view demonstrations of the "softer" emotions as weakness. This is why when women cry at work, men have such a strongly adverse reaction. Men are taught not to cry (regardless of the reason for the tears), as it is shown as a lack of control of emotions, and, therefore, a weakness. Women tend to be passionate about what they do. Men tend to have the attitude of "you just do what you have to do." When working in an environment that is 7 percent female and 93 percent male, the contrast between the gender archetypes is placed under a magnifying glass, so that when a woman gets angry and cries at work it is taken as a sign that she is not capable of doing the work.

This is the attitude that leads to one of the most enlightening conversations I have had in my career; "enlightening" because it helped me to understand what some men see when a woman behaves, well, like a woman. I was told that "women let being a woman get in the way of being a good engineer" because we are too emotional, too sensitive (to the types of comments I discuss in the previous section on professionalism), and not willing to dirty our manicured hands. You may find this surprising, but in a way, I am happy that the particular engineer who told me this (a middle-aged male, and the same one who alluded to spanking me after I was married) actually said it in so many words. At least he had the decency to say how he really feels instead of pretending to be completely unbiased and liberated while clearly suffering from an opposite mindset.

I have learned over many years that I cannot expect to be myself and be taken seriously in the workplace. I have to be just as interested in wrenches and gears as the men, regardless of where my true interest lies. I have to be willing to inject myself, interrupt conversations, and advocate aggressively for a position, even though I know that when I do that, the negative connotations of a female in the workplace are brought to mind. Essentially, what I've learned is that I'm damned if I do and damned if I don't. This makes STEM look so utterly appealing to our graduating classes, doesn't it?

You might think that all of the above makes me less motivated, and to a certain extent, you would be right. However, and I emphasize this point, I've also learned that if I'm not going to be treated as part of the team regardless of what I do, then I'm going to be my unbridled self, and if my coworkers don't like it, then they can deal with it. I have started to go to work to do a good job, not to be liked. Of course, in a way, this is also pretending because I am a people pleaser at heart and wholeheartedly want to be liked. I have turned out to be a better actor as an engineer than I might have been had I chosen acting for a career—all because I am one of the 7 percent.

BIG BIOLOGICAL TRUTHS

*"When the whole world is silent, even
one voice becomes powerful."*

—MALALA YOUSAFZAI

THERE ARE MULTIPLE misconceptions about women in the sciences. I feel these are especially true about female engineers, particularly those in the nuclear industry. As is customary on the journey we're sharing, let's talk about some of those misconceptions!

Female engineers are lesbians.

I am not a lesbian. I have been physically attracted to women, but I have never had a sexual relationship with a woman. I don't think I would necessarily avoid a sexual relationship with a woman (I think there would probably be a lot of benefits to that type of relationship, actually), but I am not primarily attracted to women.

I am attracted to men. I like sex with men. A lot. That said, I have only had four consensual sexual relationships: the one when I was sixteen, one with Melvin after my rape (ill-advised, and an admitted attempt to feel that I wasn't "damaged goods"), one with my college boyfriend, David, and one with my now-husband.

When people imply that female engineers are lesbians, this is not only offensive to women of all sexual identities, but also shows a gross misunderstanding of the type of environment most women experience in male-dominated workplaces. I'm almost certain that female engineers who are in the LGBTQ community wouldn't feel comfortable being "out" in the kind of environments I have worked in. I say this because I fall into the socially-acceptable presentation of the female gender in moderately conservative work environments, and I can't even bring my full self to work. Another instance where women are "damned if we do and damned if we don't."

When people make such statements, they always imply the most stereotypical archetype of this spectrum. By that, I mean the woman who is "manly." The irony here is that women in engineering, particularly in my chosen specialty, are looked down on if we don't have masculine interests. If we don't like to get our hands dirty, tear apart an engine on the weekend, or build electronics on our time off, then we're not "real" engineers. In one overheard conversation, this entire idea was encapsulated in a question and response I overheard at work one day:

```
Supervisor 1 (over the cube wall to Supervi-
sor 2): "Do real engineers wear nail polish?"

Supervisor 2 (back over the wall to Supervi-
sor 1): "Not in my experience."
```

Fascinating, isn't it, how we have created this ideal female engineer who is feminine (but not too feminine), has "masculine" interests, doesn't wear makeup (but also looks well put together), wears practical clothes (but still manages to look feminine), and generally embodies all the lauded female traits while not being "too girly?" How is any woman to stack up to this? Also, won't it be nice when we reach a point as a society where we stop stereotyping others?

Female engineers are "frigid" and do not enjoy sex.

I enjoy sex (surprising, given my sexual history). I enjoy sex with men, and I really enjoy sex with myself. I love the anticipation of sex, the building tension in the body, the eventual release (i.e., I love orgasms!). I love how my body responds to sexual excitement. I love how easily aroused I am, how my body so easily lubricates itself for the act of sex, and I even enjoy the way my body smells when it is aroused.

Women were taught for centuries that the female body was not supposed to have an odor (and by body, I mean the vagina). When first created, Lysol was used as a douche to help with the "dirty" smell of a woman's vagina (if you don't believe me, Google it). It was also marketed as a form of birth control! In later years, talcum powder was marketed as something to cover female odors. Of course, this use of talcum powder has now led to multiple cases of cervical cancer. That "dirty" smell is why men love to smell a woman's panties. It's the smell of sex, the smell of arousal, and it is sexy in the most fecund way. It is the smell of fertility. A woman's vagina is not supposed to smell like flowers. It is meant to smell like a vagina. Most men find this smell intoxicating (check out *50 Shades of Gray* for a hint of this, or *Perfume* for a more extreme personification) and intensely enjoy going down on a woman because of the smell and taste.

Female scientists are unattractive.
Attractive women are unintelligent.

Unfortunately, one of my favorite shows did little to negate this misconception. *The Big Bang Theory* featured an air-headed, but gorgeous Penny and two glasses-wearing, nerdy female scientists, Bernadette and Amy. Now, these characters definitely experienced growth and development over the seasons, but the caricature of the stereotypical sex bomb and nerdy girl does little to help women to be taken seriously.

I happen to wear glasses and self-identify as a nerd. But I've worked with female engineers who are exceptionally feminine, as well as ones who are very much tomboys. I feel quite attractive. I enjoy being who I am, and I try very hard to avoid conforming to any of the supposed norms that women are to obey in the arena of STEM.

I recently decided to Google "female engineer memes," hoping to find a meme to capture what people think I do (something akin to a NASA scientist) versus what I actually do (sit in front of a computer 99.99% of the time and go out into a hot power plant 0.01% of the time). Imagine my anger and disgust when I saw memes with themes such as the following in the very top results:

- Caption: Expectation (*picture of sexy blonde in a hardhat*) versus reality (*picture of a dumpy, overweight brunette in a hardhat and safety vest*).
- Caption: "What does a Female engineer do?" (*picture of several women in hardhats and white lab coats next to a picture showing the assembly of a sandwich made to look like an architectural drawing*)
- Caption: Definitely not an engineer. (*picture of an attractive brunette with a beautiful smile*)
- Caption: "When you're the only female in a class of engineers?" (*picture of a woman with approximately ten hotdogs shoved in her mouth*)

If you don't know how the Google algorithm works, it's worth stating that the algorithm is based on popularity and what you like to see. It's far from being free of bias. These memes are memes that people have decided that they enjoy looking at, are memes that are popular. This means that the majority of people searching for memes about female engineers think these memes are funny, even if they don't think they're accurate. Something tells me these memes are far more amusing to men than to the women they mock.

Pregnancy tests work immediately after intercourse.

NOT TRUE! It would be nice if this were true. Then the process could be stopped with the morning-after pill even before the egg implants and potentially becomes viable (more on "potentially" in a bit). Pregnancy tests rely on hormonal changes to detect pregnancy. They can work as early as four weeks. But even if you get a positive result at four weeks, most doctors will not see you until eight weeks. This is when doctors feel comfortable verifying the pregnancy with the first images.

There is also a lot of general misinformation (at best) and downright ignorance (at worst) about female biology. How sad for a planet where over half the population is, in fact, female, that we still consider women to be tiny men with breasts. This misinformation is rampant surrounding the discussions on abortion, and many people believe that conception happens immediately after the act of vaginal sex. But sperm can live in the vagina and uterus up to seven days. Therefore, fertilization of the egg can occur any time up to seven days after intercourse. This still doesn't constitute conception, which doesn't take place until the egg implants into the uterus. The fertilized egg cannot develop into a baby without implanting into the uterus, where it receives its nutrients.

A woman stops menstruating when she is pregnant (hence waiting for one's period).

This is another one that is not true. Many women have periods, from spotting to normal, heavy bleeding all the way through their pregnancies. This is why some girls don't know they're pregnant. Some women don't have periods at all, particularly when they're on the pill, so they don't have this indicator either. Which leads us to our next piece of misinformation....

Women can't get pregnant on the pill.

No one wants to hear this, but the pill is not effective for everyone. Not to mention "the pill" is a misnomer. There are many times of pills—better referred to as hormonal birth control. Some are estrogen; some estrogen-progesterone. Some pills are effective for one woman while they are ineffective for others. Every woman's body is different. A woman can get pregnant, and successfully carry a baby to term even if she is on the pill. This isn't common, but it's common enough. In fact, up to 8 percent of women get pregnant every year while on the pill.

The morning-after pill is the same as an abortion.

There is an abortion pill. It is known as RU486. It is not the same thing as the morning-after pill. The abortion pill terminates an existing pregnancy. The morning-after pill *helps* prevent a pregnancy from occurring. If a woman is already pregnant and takes the morning-after pill, nothing will happen to the fetus. The abortion pill is one of three options that are categorized as "medical" or "early" abortions. These are procedures that can be undertaken as soon as a pregnancy is confirmed. The abortion pill is FDA-approved to be used for up to forty-nine days after the first day of a woman's menstrual period. In other words, a woman would be seven weeks pregnant or five weeks since conception. If a woman is farther along in their pregnancy, a medical abortion may be contraindicated.

The morning-after pill will not terminate a pregnancy if implantation of the egg into the uterus has already occurred. The morning-after pill (also called plan B®) is a one-pill dose. It is meant to be taken within seventy-two hours but is more effective if taken within twelve hours after a contraceptive accident, unprotected sex, or rape. It *can* prevent pregnancy by doing one of three things via the hormones contained within the pill. It either temporarily stops the release of an egg from the ovary, prevents fertilization of an egg already released, or prevents an already-fertilized egg from attaching to the uterus.

The birth control pill causes abortions.

This is not true. Hormonal birth control (the pill, some IUDs that contain hormones, or the vaginal birth control ring) typically works in three ways although it is a little different if the method is pro-gestin only. The first way the pill can work to prevent pregnancy is to prevent growth of the uterine lining (i.e., causing the uterine lining to become thinner). Thinner uterine lining *may* lower the chances of implantation. Hormonal birth control can also work by stopping ovulation. Therefore, there is no egg that the sperm can fertilize. Hormonal birth control also thickens the mucus on the cervix, meaning sperm are less likely to be able to enter the uterus to meet up with an egg released during ovulation. An abortion is defined as the disruption of an implanted, fertilized egg. There-fore, hormonal contraceptives (like the pill or the morning-after pill) cannot terminate a pregnancy. There is no conclusive evidence indicating that the pill will harm a baby once the egg has implanted and begun to develop. That is why the pill is not always effective at preventing a pregnancy.

Conception and pregnancy are the same thing.

According to established medical knowledge, conception does not equal pregnancy. Conception is when the egg is fertilized by the sperm. Pregnancy is when the fertilized egg implants into the lining of the uterus. The egg cannot develop without being implanted into the uterine lining. That is where the blood and nutrients come from to enable the egg to develop into a viable fetus. In addition, just because the egg has implanted, that does not mean the egg is viable and will develop properly. Most pregnancies are naturally terminated by the body within the first four to six weeks as part of a woman's period.

A rape kit performs an abortion (also known as a D&C).

This statement was famously made by Texas Republican Jodie Laubenberg: "In the emergency room, they have what's called rape kits where a woman can get cleaned out." This is probably what of the most infuriating and saddening statements I have ever heard, primarily because it was said by a woman. How can a woman be so ignorant of how her own body and the procedures that affect it work? To link a rape kit to a D&C is insane.

As I am painfully aware, from personal experience, a rape kit performs an exam of the woman's body (not just her vagina) for evidence of sexual contact. Her mouth is swabbed if she has been sodomized, her vagina is swabbed if she has been vaginally penetrated by her rapists penis (doesn't do much good if it was an object rape), her anus is swabbed if he penetrated her anus with his penis (again, not much good if it was an object rape), her body is photographed if there are marks, and her nails are scraped for skin if she scratched or even touched her assailant. The vaginal swab does not penetrate into the uterus like a D&C would. A D&C dilates the cervix so that a tool can be inserted into the uterus to scrape away the uterine lining, which removes the implanted egg from the uterus (an abortion). This uterine lining and the egg or fetus are then sucked out. D&Cs are done after many miscarriages as it stops the bleeding of the thickened uterine lining that resulted from the implantation of the egg and the pregnancy hormones.

All of these mistakes and misconceptions go a long way to perpetuating the myths about women's intelligence and the ways their body functions. In fact, there's still a huge stigma around the way the female reproductive cycle occurs. We have to stop being so grossed out by the female body and so condescending about the women who choose to go into the sciences. I guess it's easier for men to assume the women going into STEM are "men with breasts and vaginas" because then they're less threatening?

I continue to read books like *Rage Becomes Her* and *Everyday Sexism* and the only conclusion I can come to is that men are terrified of, horrified by, threatened by an empowered woman because their fantastical version of power will be forever ripped from their mind and their real lives, real power, will be tremendously downsized.

CHAPTER 3

SOCIETY

IN PROTEST OF THE PINK TAX

*"I like me better naked. I don't mean that in a vain way…
When you put clothes on, you immediately put a character
on. Clothes are adjectives, they are indicators. When you don't
have any clothes on, it's just you, raw, and you can't hide."*

—Padma Lakshmi

YOU PROBABLY DON'T know me. I am not famous; not a celebrity nor in the C-suite of some multi-million- (or billion-) dollar company. I haven't been on TV, and I've never written a book before. Now that I've told you what I am not, let me tell you what I am. I am an engineer working in the nuclear power industry. I am also a woman who has experienced the subtle discrimination, the lack of representation, and the "good old boy" network that is part and parcel of this industry (and a huge reason that there isn't more female participation in it). I am also a woman who has experienced the harsher discrimination that women can inflict on other women. I have experienced rape, and I have lost a friend to suicide. I am a woman, first and foremost.

Countless remarkable books on female leadership have hit the shelves—physical and cyber. One of the most famous in the past few years was *Lean In*, by Sheryl Sandberg. Sandberg relates several instances from her own career that highlight the lingering inequalities for women in the workplace. Women like Sheryl Sandberg have paved the way for women like me to be accepted in male-dominated workplaces without being like a man. But Sandberg's main premise is still that women need to be less like women to be taken seriously in a male-dominated work environment. We need to be more confident, we need to overcome our self-limiting behaviors, and we need to, well… lean in. But that only goes so far.

Women's so-called "self-limiting" behaviors, such as not speaking up in meetings and not advocating for ourselves in performance reviews, are so ingrained to our human nature that, while we can improve them, I don't think we can ever fully overcome them. Even for those women who do have more confidence and who present themselves in a more straightforward manner, it has been proven in several research studies that they are considered unpleasant, bossy, and aggressive. So, it seems to me that without a radical shift, women are *screwed* either way (yes, I used that word on purpose).

Consider women's dress and the way we present ourselves physically. If a woman is physically attractive (and slender), she isn't taken seriously. Watch Fox News and look at the gorgeous and heavily made-up women, all of whom are highly educated, and tell me whether you take them more or less seriously than someone like Greta Van Susteren. Now, before you get all upset and thing I'm picking on Greta (which I am not, I assure you, as I think all women are beautiful and should be celebrated for it), think about the point I am making. The Fox News female anchors are classically beautiful, but do you take them seriously? Greta Van Susteren is not classically beautiful, but do you take her more seriously? And how does this compare to how you rate a male anchor's (attractive or not) qualifications?

Fox News has been repeatedly called out for its sexism, and for good reason. The women are all in sleeveless dresses with their hair perfectly coiffed and their makeup perfectly (and did I mention, heavily?) applied. The only woman I know of on Fox who is allowed to wear slacks is Maria Bartiromo. The rest of them are practically forced to wear dresses, which, as far as I am concerned, hyper-feminizes them, and makes them more of a contrast—deliberately so—to their male co-anchors. Now, that said, I don't think all of the male anchors are sexist or misogynistic, but the picture painted isn't particularly "equal." Get some of the men out there in skirts and heels, and then we're getting somewhere. Okay, so that probably isn't going to happen (though there is a straight man in Germany, I believe, who does exactly this), but I hope you take my point.

If we look at the flip side of this, a woman who dresses "like a man" in a polo shirt or collared button-down shirt and slacks, is considered to be "butch," particularly if she is overweight and wears her hair short. This is also far from a fair assessment. But a man is considered to be just as masculine whether he wears business-casual or a three-piece suit. Women are also worried about how much makeup we wear. We don't want to appear overly made-up, but we also don't want to look like we just dragged ourselves in. Studies show that men like it when women look put together, but men don't understand what it takes for us to look "put together." There's an excellent chapter in Joanne Lipman's *That's What She Said: What Men Need to Know (and Women Need to Tell Them) about Working Together* that explains what women go through to be taken seriously, but not considered too attractive, every day when we go to work.

Lipman also mentions the "pink tax," which is the phenomenon where women pay more for our clothes and personal grooming items than men do. A woman's button-down blouse is up to 60 percent more expensive than a man's shirt based on my personal experience. And that's if you can even find one that fits and doesn't gape at the chest (not a good way to be taken seriously at work). Women's deodorant, hair products, shaving gel, and even razors are more expensive than men's, too, even when they contain the same ingredients or have the same number of blades. What is up with that? If you're a single mother raising a family, you're better off buying men's personal care products than women's if you're trying to save money!

Then there's the still-all-too-common topic of sexual harassment and out-and-out discrimination that still take place even in 2021. Women are far more likely than their male counterparts to be sexually harassed or discriminated against (unless, of course, they are a minority). Minorities of all types are still discriminated against at an unacceptable rate. This leads to the "war on white men" complaint, of course. But if you look at most company boards (including that of INPO, a nuclear information sharing organization), there's one thing most members have in common: they're old, and they're white. I'm not making this declaration to be discriminatory myself; I'm stating it as a fact.

And before we try to lay this all at (white) men's doors, like it's all their fault, let's peek at women's part in harassing and discriminating against their own gender. We all have our own unconscious biases, even me. I have judged female supervisors who were nice as "too nice" and "not effective" while judging female supervisors who managed more assertively as "aggressive" and "bitchy." I am not proud of that fact. It wasn't until reading *That's What She Said*, where Lipman admitted to her own similar biases, that I thought, *oh, no. I've done that too*. I have also been on the other side of the harassment and discrimination at one of the darkest times in my life, which I recounted earlier in this book. Women, often, instead of supporting each other in a "we're all in this together" philosophy, tend to backstab and compete with each other. It is a fact that truly saddens me.

Women are seriously underrepresented in the power industry, and particularly in nuclear. I have now worked in the nuclear power industry as a mechanical engineer for about fifteen years. In that time, there have been numerous meetings where I am the only female. A man never walks into a meeting in this industry where he is the only man. And while this book is about my experience as a female, it should be noted that there isn't much minority representation in this industry either. This isn't because of some ethnic stereotyping, it's because there just aren't as many women or other minorities in engineering. There have been many attempts to answer the "why" to that question, but no one has been meticulous in coming up with a good reason.

A lot of women who came up in the past few decades have decided that to work in a male-dominated industry, they have to be "one of the guys." I have no desire to act like one of the guys, but I can understand why women think this is their best bet in this industry for being taken seriously. The few women in the nuclear industry who have attained significant "rank" at a nuclear plant did so by "earning their stripes" (it's not an accident that the military jargon weaves its way into the nuclear industry). Consider, again, how women are told to behave in a male-dominated work force. We are told to "lean in" (I'm not picking on Sandberg either, but this is one point where she and I disagree), to be "more assertive," to "speak up for ourselves." The similarity here is that all of these are predominantly male traits. So, essentially, for a woman to be successful in a male-dominated industry, she is advised to act like a male. I rebel against this thought, and I think it's time for men to start coming to the table and frankly, acting more like women, so that we can meet at the intersection of true equality.

As these words and ideas grind in, I hope to elicit understanding. That is the first step toward realizing that STEM, engineering, and the nuclear industry can be changed for the better to help us be a more diversified discipline. Once there is understanding about what a woman's experience actually is, in both life and the nuclear industry, then perhaps we can start the slow process of change. It starts with family members, even grandparents.

GRANDMA AND GAL PALS

*"There is a special place in hell for women
who don't help other women."*

—MADELEINE ALBRIGHT

ONE OF THE most disappointing things that I have discovered
in my life (not just limited to my career) is that some of the most
sexist people are women and that their sexism isn't directed to
men (something that might be understandable) but against other
women. Sometimes this sexism is rather innocuous and can be seen
in the following attitudes of some women:

- "A woman wouldn't make a good president because she's
  too vulnerable."
- "A woman doesn't make a good supervisor because she
  wants to be everyone's friend."
- "A wife can't be raped because she's supposed to have sex
  with her husband."

These are all things I have heard said by women, and on the face
of things, these attitudes seem somewhat harmless because they're
attitudes held by mothers or grandmothers—older generations
that just don't always seem to "get things." But these attitudes have
seeped into the very fiber of society. They affect how we raise girls
on a subconscious level. We limit women from their very inception
into womanhood because they're already told there are some things

in life they can't do or must expect to experience, and that's fuck-ing wrong.

My grandmother on my dad's side made the third comment above. This was in relation to a news article she had read about a man who was arrested for raping his wife. She was completely confused as to how that could be a crime, since a woman's job was to have sex with her husband whenever he wanted it—oh, and to conceive and bear him a son while she was at it. I don't remem-ber what arguments I used with my grandmother on that topic. I might have changed the subject, knowing that, like with many other topics, the argument I gave wouldn't make a difference in the end. Some people are so ingrained to their beliefs that no argument and no amount of proof to the contrary can ever alleviate them of their beliefs. This is a phenomenon referred to as *religious fervor*.

My mother actually made the first statement above. She believes firmly that women's liberation has hurt women more than any other women's rights movement in history. She thinks that women have decided to act like men in their promiscuity and their foul mouths and that it has hurt women. Sadly, I don't think she's entirely wrong. Women's liberation (and no, I wasn't there in the 60s to experience it, while my mother was) used men as the rubric to pattern women's habits upon. Men were the rulers of the world—and still are… we sincerely haven't come as far as we might like to think—and governed society. Men were sexually free, aggres-sive, and when they dropped f-bombs, were taken more seriously. In essence, women decided that's what they needed to do to be respected. And sadly, I do think that set us back.

Because women decided that to be taken seriously in a man's world and to be included in men's industries they must act just like the men, we've perpetuated a hyper-masculinized society. Watch a show like *Suits* or *Billions* and watch how the women in those firms act. They are "ballsy," "aggressive," and "take charge" women, and we women that watch those shows eat them up. And we miss the lesson 100% of the time. I'm not saying women are supposed to be the softer sex and prance around in petticoats and corsets. Far from it. What I'm saying is there should be a place for kindness in the workplace without women being disrespected and considered weak.

And weak is what we are considered, unless we act like a total bitch in the workplace, and while that might get us grudging respect, it's not the same respect that the men capture. Consider the following tired phrases that we hear all the time:

- "You run like a girl."
- "He screamed like a little girl."
- "You throw like a girl."

Those aren't statements of praise; they are implications that someone is effeminate, womanly, less-than-effective. How insulting! When after reading Lipman's book I had the brutal gut-punch sensation that I, myself, have participated in this anti-female attitude, I immediately decided that I would be more aware of my judgmental attitudes toward women and focus on empowering them. I would reset my own narrative. After all, how can I expect to be empowered myself if I am participating in the same bullshit in which I am being critical?

BURN HAZARD

*"If we don't change, we don't grow. If we
don't grow, we aren't really living."*

—Gail Sheehy

WE'VE ALL HEARD about "rape culture," but what does that mean, exactly? And what, if anything, does it have to do with gender parity in male-dominated workplaces? Well, let's examine it further and see.

Rape culture is a term that first came to prominence in the 1970s. It was coined by feminists of this era and was meant to highlight the tendency of society to blame survivors of sexual assault and normalize male sexual violence. A Google search of the term "rape culture" brings up many listings. Scanning the top few, and clicking on the links, I am led to the following information:

- On the website *www.wavaw.ca*, there is a really good discussion of rape culture. The website states that many feminists have provided their own definition of rape culture. For example, the website states that Emilie Buchwald, author of *Transforming a Rape Culture*, defines rape culture as: "a complex set of beliefs that encourage male sexual aggression and supports violence against women. It is a society where violence is seen as sexy and sexuality as violent. In a rape culture, women perceive a continuum of threatened violence that ranges from sexual remarks to sexual touching to rape itself. A rape culture condones physical and emotional terrorism against women as the norm . . . In a rape culture both men and women assume that sexual violence is a fact of life, inevitable."

- The website *www.southern.edu* has an entire page devoted to rape culture, showing their concern for and trying to educate their student body. Southern's page defines rape culture as "an environment in which rape is prevalent and in which sexual violence is normalized and excused in the media and popular culture." They go further in saying that "Rape culture is perpetuated through the use of misogynistic language, the objectification of women's bodies, and the glamorization of sexual violence, thereby creating a society that disregards women's rights and safety." Southern's page also gives some great examples of what rape culture is, including: "Blaming the victim ("She asked for it!"), trivializing sexual assault ("Boys will be boys!"), tolerance of sexual harassment, inflating false rape report statistics, and teaching women to avoid getting raped." There are many more examples they cite, and I highly recommend viewing their page for more information. They even go further and define "victim blaming" and explain why it is so dangerous.
- Wikipedia also has an article on the subject. They discuss the history of the term and list some behaviors that are commonly associated with rape culture, such as: victim blaming, slut-shaming, sexual objectification, trivializing rape, denial of widespread rape, refusing to acknowledge the harm caused by sexual violence, or some combination of these.

Note that "tolerance of sexual harassment" is included as an example of what rape culture is. Sexually explicit jokes are another example, as are sexually related statements. Sadly, I've experienced this in my career. The first instance was shortly after I began working. A bold co-worker, an electrical designer, said that he'd "never been spanked by a girl as cute as me." Your first thought might be "That's a random statement." And you would be right. There was no lead-up to it. That's just what he said after being introduced to me. Your second thought might be "It's a weird comment, so it's not worth considering." That's where you'd be wrong. As long as men think they can talk like that to women at work, they'll continue to treat us like second-class citizens. My next experience is a good example of this.

I was working closely with a male engineer on a calculation at one point. The work involved many phone and instant messenger conversations, since we worked in offices in different states, even though we both worked for the same company. This male engineer was older and had been in the nuclear industry a long time. He hadn't worked with many women, for that reason, and clearly expected women to adapt themselves to the male work environment if they wanted to work as engineers. This may seem a reasonable expectation, except the male work environment at the time he began his career involved the posting of explicit, pornographic images throughout the power plant, including on the door to the control room. I know this because of tales from men and women who used to work in the industry. But it featured strongly in a story he told me about a woman who worked with him during that era.

This woman was a "good engineer" because she would march up to the control room door, place her hand right on the "pussy" of the woman who was "spread open" in the centerfold pasted to the door of the control room (and, yes, this was a conversation he had with me over the phone at work). If anyone reading this thinks that's an environment any person (female or not) should be subjected to or that the woman should get any less respect if she complained about that centerfold, then perhaps you should reevaluate your beliefs. This was the same engineer that went on to tell me that women didn't make good engineers because they "let being a woman get in the way of being a good engineer." What he meant was that we're too sensitive to the "male environment."

This engineer is also the one who routinely called me "babe," "sweetheart," and "honey." He would send me hearts through Instant Messenger. All of which I tolerated because I already knew (from his story above) that I would be retaliated against if I complained. I knew that if I complained I'd be considered "too sensitive." And I knew that he was the type that would then withhold information that I needed to do my job. I had already complained about the use of the word "pussy" at work. He used it twice in the same phone call. I'd had to take that complaint to the project engineer. He sent out an email reminding people about proper language and behavior in the workplace. All that did was prompt a "Why are people so sensitive?" discussion from this engineer, so what expectation did I have that he would hear any of my other complaints?

The highlight of my interaction with this engineer came when we were finishing up work on the calculation and he made the following comment: "If you weren't married, I'd spank your ass right now." This comment was written in an instant message at work. So, you can see that he clearly did not "get it" and understand that this was improper behavior.

I had finally had enough and was close to the point where I didn't need his help anymore. I reported his comment to my boss, who also happened to be a female. She was visibly grossed out by the comment. She knew this engineer; everyone did because he was the subject matter expert for our hydraulic calculation software and facilitated all the training. This guy was no looker and smoked like a chimney. Of all the men to be hit on by, he was probably the most disturbing prospect. She asked if I wanted it elevated up the management chain, and I said "yes." She knew I'd been putting up with a lot and fully understood why I was keeping mum about it.

She informed her supervisor and the mechanical chief engineer. It was reported to HR and went through all the official channels. But then it fell flat.

Very recently in my career, there have been more inappropriate comments and harassing behavior. This behavior has not been directed at me but is more evident of a systemic issue in the company. That said, it's still unacceptable. When I reported the incidents to HR, I was asked if I had discussed these issues with my supervisory chain. I cited the example from my previous job where the chief engineer had told me that the harassing behavior I had reported was a result of the engineer just being "the way he is." I told them I'd already learned in my career that I couldn't trust my management chain.

Sexual harassment is still alive and well in corporate America, and, as we've established, this is a symptom of a rape culture. Until we can correct this culture, we can't hope for sexual harassment to truly end, which will lead to more and more women either not complaining because they know it will do no good or leaving the workforce because they just can't stand the behavior anymore. Why is it we can't get past this? Why is rape culture so prevalent?

I think the main reason for its prevalence is that men don't understand what rape is for a woman. So, let's talk again about that in this safe space. Let's talk again about what sex is like for a woman versus a man. It bears repeating because this is in important topic and repetition is key when you're trying to drive home a point.

Women are always the ones penetrated during sex; men are always the ones doing the penetrating. Now, there are rare sex games and S&M activities involving artificial anatomy, but that is not what we are talking about. We're talking about conventional sexual activity. Women's bodies are always "violated" during the sex act, while men's are always "violating." Most people look at sex as simply a pleasurable activity between consenting adults. And when it is, it is a wonderful experience, but one that women naturally consider more emotional than men do, since their bodies are being *entered*.

Rape, though, is the sex act gone wrong. It has nothing to do with love or desire in the traditional sense, as between a loving couple. It becomes an act of domination and power. It simply manifests as the sex act. And due to the nature of sex between a man and a woman, it is so much more a violation because the penetration is now forced instead of being accepted and welcomed through an act of consent. The notion of having foreign DNA injected into one's vagina by a forcible sexual act makes most women physically ill. This is completely converse to the desire a female might feel for a man with whom she wants to have a one-night stand.

Again, rape is about power and domination. Many women are physically weaker than their sexual partners just by the default of biology. It is easy for a woman to be overpowered by their partner. Many women live in constant fear that an act of consensual sex can turn violent and that they would not be able to defend themselves. It is the ultimate act of trust for a woman to consent to sex with a man or another woman, depending on the nature of the encounter.

We have this misconception that rape is about dark alleys, men jumping out from behind bushes, women getting beaten or slashed up by a Jack the Ripper, or object rape. But rape can be far more insidious than that. Acquaintance rape, date rape, is one of those types of rape. It is almost always a he-said, she-said situation. There is seldom any physical evidence that one can point to. There is ejaculate (unless a condom was used). There can be abrasions on the vagina, but these can be due to consensual sex, as well. There have been several episodes of shows like *Law and Order: Special Victims Unit* and *CSI* where it is implied that the location of the abrasions on the vagina can be linked to rape, but I have found no evidence of this being true in all cases of rape. Recall, also, that a woman can be aroused during rape, as well. The body's physiological responses do not always align with the body's physical responses.

I should take the opportunity here to mention that these things did not happen to my body when I was raped. However, they do happen to some women. Just because an act is non-consensual doesn't mean the body doesn't have a physical response to it. That is one of the hardest things to understand about rape. Many surmise if it's non-consensual, then you don't experience any pleasure at all. That is simply not true. Some women can even orgasm during rape. Now, many women are slow to orgasm, and have to be in the right mindset in order to achieve it; all the stars have to align. But for other women, it happens very easily; even during a nightmare scenario, as counter intuitive as that might sound.

Date rape also seems to bring the most invasive questions. What were you wearing? What did you say to indicate that you wanted sex? Did you say no forcibly? Did you push him away? If a man grabs a woman on the street and pulls her into a back alley, rapes her, and physically assaults her, there is far more sympathy for the woman raped (note, I do not use the word "victim" here, as "victim" implies weakness, and a woman who is raped is not weak). That's not to say there isn't some blame attached to the woman who was raped. The question of what a woman was wearing to "encourage" the rape always seems to come up. No one ever asks what the rapist was wearing, though. Shirtless? Tight jeans accentuating their big bulge?

Why can't a woman be allowed to dress for herself, to dress sexily, without it being an invitation for a man to rape her? I get that men are "visual creatures," (as if women aren't), but there is such a thing as self-control. Women enjoy sex, so why can't they enjoy feeling sexy and physically attractive? Do we have to start dressing women like they do in fundamentalist countries or as the handmaids are dressed in the wildly successful show, *A Handmaid's Tale*, to remove the culpability that women always seem to have in their own assaults? Does a woman need to record every sexual encounter to be able to prove her rape or to protect herself from the threat of a rape? When will men take responsibility for their own sexual responses the way women have been forced to since the beginning of time?

Some of the most pervasive phrasing in our society concerns being "screwed over." This is phrased in many ways: fucked, fucked over, shafted, forced to bend over and take it, bent over a barrel. One of my least favorite new phrases is "butt hurt." Now, I guarantee no one who uses these phrases thinks that they are participating in rape culture but let me explain the correlation.

The majority of these phrases originated in the male-dominated business world where if a business deal did not go right, someone had been "shafted." I would wager (though I don't think I can find proof of this) that all of these phrases originated with men for the sheer fact that sexual violence is the biggest fear that women have. We don't joke about that shit. We look over our shoulder when we walk to our car at night, whether we're at the grocery store or leaving a bar. Some women refrain from taking Ubers or cabs alone if the driver is male. Though sadly, they're not guaranteed safety anymore if the driver is female, as many females who "recruit" for the sex trafficking circles are themselves survivors of abuse and feel they have to bring other women in if for no other reason than to spare themselves from continuing rape and torture.

The male-dominated business world has been shown in recent history to be one of hyper masculinity (characterized by aggressive language, homophobia, and obsessive fear with showing weakness). Interesting, isn't it, that predominantly homophobic and even closeted men who don't dare come out in the office would joke about something like this? By "something like this" I mean the topic of a non-consensual sex act with a man. If ignorance still lingers as to the meaning of this phrase, after all this, I'm about to destroy illusions. I'm talking about anal sex: specifically, an act of rape that is predominately a male-on-male act.

Think about it… This phrase likely originated with men expressing being taken advantage of in a business deal. To what else could it be referring? These aren't new phrases ("butt hurt" is the newest iteration) and have been around in many forms as long as men have dominated the business world. Why would you phrase a business situation in terms of non-consensual sex? What makes a straight man think that a joke like that is appropriate? Male-on-male rape is the biggest fear men have when going to prison, so I ask again, WHY WOULD YOU JOKE ABOUT THAT?

The fact that these phrases are so prevalent in our society shows a disturbing tolerance for "rape language." In fact, these phrases have come to be synonymous with non-consensual sex with a woman in which she is anally penetrated or vaginally penetrated from behind. Regardless of what gender the phrase is being used about, the connotation is one of non-consensual sex in an *extremely dominant position* by the penetrator. The act is an orgy of power and domination for the perpetrator. Sex performed in this position is one that puts the person being penetrated in an extremely precarious situation if the act is violent. It is virtually impossible to fight when face down. You can struggle (which is the point), but you can do very little real damage to the rapist in that position.

So, if you've used any of these phrases, you've participated in rape culture. I admit to using these phrases before (I have even used them in this book) and not really thinking about what they mean. Not the literal meaning, but the more cultural meaning; the acceptance that it implies for an act that should never be tolerated. I have to try to police my own language and to tactfully correct others when they use these phrases.

One older, white, straight male in my office uses the phrase "butt hurt" a lot. Several other men use the terms "screwed over" and even "fucked over" when they feel like they can use a real four-letter word in "mixed company." I know they know what these terms mean, but we've become so very desensitized to it because of the prevalence. If someone was out and out talking about rape in the office, people would be uncomfortable. Well, at least you'd think so.

I have one example from my office that belies that point, so perhaps the problem is even more severe than I want to acknowledge.

During the Brett Kavanaugh hearings, rape was a big topic. What constituted consent? What was an improper relationship? When did an improper relationship become a sexual assault? A perfect example of this dilemma was the Clinton / Lewinski situation. Had this happened in today's era of #MeToo, this would have seized more attention in a completely different way. President Bill Clinton was the most powerful man in the free world. Yet there was very little said about him using his position to solicit an improper relationship with Monica Lewinsky. Honestly, what could Monica have done if she'd refused him, and he'd fired her? He could have blackballed her. She might never have been able to work again, especially in politics. But instead of blaming Clinton, we blamed Monica for being a "slut," a "whore," a girl who was infatuated with Bill Clinton and, according to some people's opinion, practically forced herself on *him*.

These were the types of conversations that surrounded the Kavanaugh hearings. Two of my coworkers, one of whom sat in the cubicle adjacent to mine at the time, are very conservative. Think MAGA, Trump support, and all the bad stereotypes that come along with conservative views in our current culture. One of them was talking about an instance when he was at boys' camp as a child. He said something along the lines of "The older boy who was roughhousing around with me wasn't a bad kid when things went 'too far', just like the father who put the moves on my [couldn't hear this part] in the car on the way home when she was sixteen and babysitting for his kids wasn't a bad guy. Sometimes things just happen. It doesn't make it *rape*."

WHAT THE FUCK was even going on with this conversation? I could tell the other guy was uncomfortable. He wanted to agree but couldn't quite bring himself to. I was left sitting there torn between compassion for this man who had certainly been molested by a boy who was probably his camp counsellor, based on the context of the conversation, and pure rage that he could think a father hitting on a sixteen-year-old babysitter didn't make him a "bad guy." While I realize that part of his logic was trying to normalize and justify something that happened to him as a child and that he probably didn't get counselling for, there is no excuse for feeling up a teenage girl if you're a father of a child she is babysitting and you're giving her a ride home.

But this is another aspect of rape culture. We don't acknowledge sexual assault or rape much of the time for what it is, so we try to justify, excuse, and normalize the behaviors. If a girl is sixteen and you're the father of the child she's babysitting, if you grope her THAT IS ASSAULT and if you put your hand down her pants THAT IS RAPE. There is no justification for that. If a girl is drunk and you do either of those things to her, or if she works for you and you exert power over whether she keeps her job and you do either of those things to her, they are ASSAULT and RAPE, respectively. Why do men have to be told this? How can they not know?

I told my supervisor about this discussion, and he fed it back to his peers and his boss. The other supervisors then had "training" sessions with their direct reports to discuss why this conversation wasn't appropriate. I recently found out from a woman who was in one of these other groups that the exact wording her supervisor used was, "I have to give this training because someone on our floor is 'too sensitive'."

Recently at work, I've had two instances of inappropriate language that would probably seem innocuous and might even be funny outside the workplace. In one instance, an ops trainer (the same one who told me not to go running out of there screaming like a little girl) stopped by my desk during a refueling outage to chat. We were talking about something where steam pressure got backed up and he said, "It basically behaved like a giant butt plug." (First of all, yuck; second of all, THIS IS AN OFFICE!) I said nothing because in a male-dominated office I already know I'd be considered too sensitive given how my feedback on the "rape discussion" had been received.

Ironically, the second instance of inappropriateness was provided by the very same supervisor who alluded to me being "too sensitive" when he was talking about a flooding scenario that every plant has to evaluate for after the Fukushima event. He said we'd all get a "douching." Again, yuck. But this is the soiled environment in which I work.

I have two nieces and I very much want them to feel empowered to go into the sciences. Given all I've laid out in this chapter, it makes it questionable for me to recommend engineering to them, much less the nuclear power industry. It makes it that much more painful for me that I'm an advocate for nuclear energy because I am emphatically not an advocate for this type of behavior. But this, too, is rape culture. And it is absolutely pervasive. Let's put a stop to it so that my nieces can feel free to pursue whatever avenue they want to without fear of being denigrated.

A DECADENT PROPOSITION

"Life shrinks or expands in proportion to one's courage."

—*Anais Nin*

IN THE FALL of 1978, Pauline Rose Clance and Suzanne Imes published an article, "The Imposter Phenomenon in High-Achieving Women: Dynamics and Therapeutic Intervention" in the journal, *Psychotherapy Theory, Research and Practice*. In this article, Clance and Imes study a group of 152 women in undergraduate and graduate programs, as well as in professional fields such as anthropology, nursing, law, and teaching. This study focused on the fact that many women have a fear of being "found out"; that they are not good enough or smart enough to succeed on their own without luck or a helping hand. Many of the women studied didn't think that their own intelligence was to be credited for their success.

I think many women still experience this. I know I do. We call it a lack of confidence or self-esteem and we tell women that they just need to "lean in" when they work in male-dominated industries. We berate women for not being more secure in themselves and in their abilities when negotiating with men for raises or promotions. Yet multiple studies show how women are graded more harshly than men in subjects such as math and computer programming. Studies also show that men are promoted based on their potential, where women are promoted based on their performance.

How are women supposed to be more confident when they

know that they'll still be judged more harshly than their male colleagues? And if women are confident, how are they supposed to then succeed when the system is stacked against them?

When I was in college, I took a computer programming class in C++. I abhorred that class! I got Fortran programming language because it was pretty easy, and you had to think like an engineer to program. But C++ with the object-oriented coding simply threw me for a loop. We had one assignment where we were supposed to create a code that would simulate the role of a die. Essentially, it had to be a random number generator that generated a random number between 1 and 6. I had been reading the textbook obsessively throughout the class hoping for some enlightenment on the topic, and I was thrilled when I found an example in the book that was almost an exact duplicate of the assignment.

I wrote my code and submitted the assignment. This was the first assignment in which I had any confidence in earning a good grade. I wasn't the only one who had realized the assignment was practically verbatim to an example in the book, so we were all feeling confident that week. When the grades were handed out, I did, in fact, get an *A*, as did the majority of the class. I was the only one, however, who was told that my code was "almost too efficient." Why weren't the men in my class also suspected of having cheated? My grades weren't that far below some of my male colleagues, and they were higher than some of the other men's grades. Why was I the only one who was selected for such a backhanded compliment?

I already felt out of place in that class. When the professor gave the impression that I basically had no expectation of getting a good grade, and that when I achieved one, I had to have come about it nefariously, I felt even more out of place. I wanted so badly to succeed, but even when I succeeded, it couldn't have been based on my own efforts. It never seemed to occur to him that an example could have been provided in the textbook that was similar to any of his assignments. Even when I mentioned that I had found a similar example in the book and showed it to him, he seemed surprised that I was able to make the connection between the example and the assignment.

My motivation definitely suffered for the rest of the semester, and I wasn't even upset when I got a *C* in that class. After all, as my friends and I joked back then "C" is for "Complete," "D" is for "Done," and "F" is for "Fuck, I have to do it again."

I wish I could say that that was the only time I was made to feel as if my efforts in my career weren't sufficient, but I would be lying if I made that assertion. There have been several notable events in my career that have made me feel inferior. The first was an incident I relayed in a previous chapter that occurred early in my career.

We had one of four projects the company was working on get cancelled. Instead of laying off the team members from the project that was cancelled, they absorbed those people into the remaining three teams. One of those teams was mine. I had been the responsible engineer for a system for several months, but when we absorbed the other personnel into my team, I was demoted from being the responsible engineer to supporting two senior male engineers. They directed the work and told me what to write, what changes to make to drawings, and what documents we needed to issue. None of the real work was mine anymore. No one had told me what I had done wrong. I had worked very hard to fix the schedule for my system. Items hadn't been well sequenced, and the order of the tasks wasn't spelled out in a way where the schedule could be effectively tracked. When I answered a question in a meeting held to discuss the changes to the schedule, my supervisor said, "Your opinion no longer matters."

I briefly mentioned an episode where I was yelled at by a manager. That was at the same company. I had been working to revise a specification for a piece of equipment that we were subcontracting. The procedure instructed me to revise the specification and provide it to the subcontract manager. What it neglected to mention was that I needed an accompanying piece of paper called a "requisition" when I provided the specification to the subcontract manager.

Now, I knew from the process of purchasing other items that weren't subcontracted that a requisition was the piece of paper that "communicated" changes between engineering and the purchasing or subcontracting departments. The subcontract procedure had a major error in eliminating the requisition process. I explained this to the subcontracts manager and told him the procedure needed to be fixed to add the form. His response was to move closer to me (he was a very tall man), point his finger in my face, and yell, "Just get me the damned requisition."

This was right in front of the quality assurance (QA) manager, a mild-mannered guy, who said nothing at all. Not even "Whoa, let's calm down, we can get this fixed."

I even went to my boss, who said, "Just do the requisition."

I sincerely replied, "What about, 'stop when unsure'?" Stop When Unsure is one of the tenants of the nuclear power industry. It means if something doesn't seem right, stop and fix it before continuing.

He barked, "You know what needs to be done, just do it."

I went back to my desk and wrote a CR (condition report). This is another thing that is a tenant of the nuclear power industry. When there is a problem with safety or a procedure, or even a potential problem, you write a CR. The threshold is low for a reason. Better to report something as an issue and find out it's not a problem (likely because there was information the CR author just didn't know existed, since they don't make documentation particularly easy to find in our industry) than for there to be an actual problem which then festers and causes a nuclear safety issue.

The CR went to the project director, a man named Charles. Charles took a look at the CR and told my project engineer, the same one I had complained to about being demoted, that the procedure didn't say "don't do a requisition."

The project engineer apparently (this conversation was relayed to me by the project engineer) said, "Charles, yes it does. It says you don't need a requisition. Doesn't even talk about one anywhere in the document."

Charles responded, "Well, that's not what it means."

My project engineer said, "Charles, you can't expect engineers to make that call. Fix the procedure."

This was another incident that made me feel out of place and inferior to the men I was surrounded by: Charles, my boss (Nar had been replaced by this time, and this boss was just as bad), my project engineer, and the QA manager. If it hadn't been for my project engineer advocating for me, I'd have been completely overrun by the organization. They thought my sole purpose in writing the CR was to embarrass them (my boss actually asked me about this), not to fix the problem.

Then there was the time that the project director (Charles had been replaced by this time) wanted to release some piping for fabrication. The process was that after the design drawings from the vendor were approved the material would be released to be fabricated. The problem was that this pipe (huge 120-inch concrete pipe) ran under a building whose weight had not been finalized. The load on the pipe, therefore, wasn't known. In addition, the load of the building dictated the differential settling between the pipe under the building and that in the yard— underground, but not physically under the building.

I refused to sign the paperwork because another principle of the nuclear power industry is "own your signature." In other words, if you don't feel comfortable signing something, don't sign it. An email was sent out by the project director, who didn't even know who I was, that blasted me to every level of management in the company saying, "Whoever this Karle person is needs to do their job and release this pipe for fabrication now."

I was mortified, hurt, and furious. I was doing my job, and no one seemed to understand that. I went into my project engineer's office and confronted him about the email. He said, "I told you to just release the pipe for fabrication."

"But we don't know the weight of the building! It's not the right thing to do!" I protested. And then, to my further mortification, I began to cry. I was balling in front of my project engineer and his good friend, my mentor at the time. To their credit, they handled it really well. But it did nothing to alleviate my utter misery. And the madder I got at myself for crying, the more I cried. In the end, we resolved the issue. My project engineer and mentor once again went to bat for me, but I learned another lesson that day: No matter how well I did my job and did what the industry standards expected of me, I would never be appreciated like the men.

In my current job, I have held two roles that were held by other engineers who had been with the company far longer than I had. Instead of talking to me about the programs that are my responsibility, people frequently go to the previous owners of these programs to ask questions. Granted, they might know the answer right off. But I'm not even given the chance to try to respond. This is a frequent problem at my office, where if you're not "known" in the organization you barely exist.

All of these things go to reinforce the feeling that I'm not "enough" at work. That I'm not smart enough or competent enough to do the job. I have moments of my inner critic ranting, *they'll eventually find out that I really don't know what I'm doing and then they'll let me go.* Intellectually, I know that isn't true. I know I'm smart, I know I'm capable. But that little niggling voice is always there at the back of my mind whispering, "You aren't enough." It was only very recently when I was turned down for yet another job I interviewed for within my company, a transfer out of my current department and into a new management structure that I had hopes would be more diverse and equitable, that it finally occurred to me: *Why would I want to work in a place that doesn't appreciate you for who you are?*

I'm not suggesting that companies change their processes full stop to address the impostor syndrome. But men and women need different mentoring to be successful. A process that involves a "meet in the middle" mentality would go a long way to helping women climb the corporate ladders in companies where diversity is a stated goal. Yes, women do need to learn to silence that voice that tells them they aren't perfect, but companies need to start providing targeted feedback, mentoring, and sponsorship that acknowledges the different strengths that women bring to the table.

POWER GLASS

"The language you are about to hear… is disturbing."

—DAVE CHAPPELLE

I SAW A fantastic meme recently. It featured a beautiful nude Medusa holding the head of Perseus. The caption stated: "Be happy we only want equality and not revenge." Powerful! (Recall in mythology that Perseus slew the Medusa, cutting off her head.)

A few men reading this are thinking *typical feminist, man-hating rhetoric*. And if it were true that the only bad things that had happened to women throughout history was a little second-class-citizen treatment, then I would agree that the meme is overkill. But that isn't all that has happened to women over the millennia. Unfortunately, there were far worse things that women had to deal with.

Shedding light on the disturbing past illuminates the present, which the majority of decent human beings want to be equitable, fair and beautiful, and what is plausible for the future, as change is the only constant in the cycle of life. I, for one, will do anything to make that change *positive*—thus, this, what I deem "power glass." You can see through it as a mirror to *you*, who you are inside and out, and your ability to transform and then help to transform others is the greatest power conceivable. Pure awareness is the first key.

Women throughout history have been considered to have less value than men. Whether it is the wage gap or the fact that women, until maybe one hundred years ago in the U.S. were considered the positions of their husbands; hence the reason they didn't need the right to vote. Even in modern times, female children have been set aside or even killed in favor of a real or potential male heir. In many ancient cultures, female children were simply left out in the wilderness to die. No, not killed outright, but left out to die of exposure or to be eaten by wild animals. A cowardly way to end a life. Many today argue about abortion and the morality of killing a baby that is still in the womb and is full-term or killing it as soon as it has been delivered, but we fail to realize that this has happened to many babies throughout history (male and female, to be fair).

Then there was the lovely task that was almost certainly left to women: killing their frail babies. If a woman gave birth to a deformed child, she was expected to kill it. In Rome, it was the law by default, since the male head of household ruled the house with an iron fist and was not considered a father unless he accepted the baby into his household. If a Roman child was born with a disability or visible malformation, the child would not be accepted, as it would be a financial burden for its entire natural life. The mother likely had two choices; smother the child or abandon it out in the open. On the shore of Israel, in an ancient city named Ashkelon, archaeologists found the remains of over one hundred babies in the city's sewers. It's believed that one out of every four Roman babies didn't make it through the first year of life.

Killing an unwanted baby or terminating an unwanted pregnancy is not new. In fact, one might argue that it is far better for a pregnancy to be terminated than for an unwanted child to be born into an unloving family. The best that can be hoped for is that the child is ignored. But how often are children beaten, starved, locked in closets, raped, or killed by parents that never should have been parents. A child is a gift, yes. But not all human beings are capable of appreciating that gift. Far better for them never to become parents, as far as I am concerned.

One wonders how many baby girls were killed because they were considered a burden to their family. Women in the past couldn't have jobs, weren't considered able to do heavy labor, and weren't allowed to contribute to society. Women were only considered to be a vessel to deliver a male heir or, better yet, multiple male children, in case one died. Since only men could own property, the only way to ensure property or a kingdom would continue in a family line was to have a male heir. Women were frequently blamed for not being able to provide a male heir. Ironically (and they had no way of knowing this back then), it is the male's sperm that dictates the gender of the baby. A lot of women were put aside in favor of another sexual partner when a male heir could not be provided.

Time to talk periods. I don't understand why men are so uncomfortable with periods. It is a natural, biological event for a woman. At least women are no longer considered unclean or untouchable during sex. In fact, now, it's the opposite. We see commercials with women prancing around in skimpy clothes or (my favorite) in white who are, apparently, simply overjoyed to have their periods. These are mythical creatures—women who are overjoyed to have their periods. I have come to accept mine, but I don't think I'll ever be at a point where I'm running around in virgin white lingerie smiling at the sun.

In many ancient cultures, women were considered to be unclean during their periods. Most cultures isolated their women in special huts when they were bleeding. Men are still, frankly, cowards when it comes to hearing about menstruation, but at least women aren't considered to be dirty or capable of souring milk, dulling a man's wits, or leading to death.

Then we have the wonderful historical obsession with virginity that's really not historical. There are many men who are still obsessed with taking a woman's virginity. There is also this obsession with pre-pubescence, I find, like the Brazilian wax. Yes, I understand how it might be nice not to have to deal with any grooming down there, but a woman's vulva is supposed to have hair on it. It provides protection for this delicate area. This obsession with bald vulvas is rather disturbing.

Some of the things they used to do to women to ensure they were "pure" when they were married are horrible. Women have never been allowed to be sexual creatures, even though science proves women enjoy sex just as much as men do, if not more. In many ancient cultures, if a man found out that his unmarried daughter had slept with a man, he could sell her into slavery—and this was completely legal. The other cultures did and still do make sure that their wives are virgins during the wedding ceremony.

A particularly disturbing example, during the wedding ceremony, the tribal chief would use his fingers to rupture the bride's hymen in front of the crowd to prove she was a virgin. Think about that. Not only is her virginity being "proven," but it's being proven for all to see! Forget the public hangings of the past, this is a public rape. That's horrific! It almost (*almost*) seems tame that in ancient Israel, any woman who lost her virginity before marriage was likely to be stoned to death.

So-called "virgin testing" still goes on in many countries. A recent article (dated August, 5 2021) states that only now is Indonesia considering repealing a law that allows the military to "virgin test" female recruits. This test is performed via the "two-finger test" method, where the doctors insert two fingers into the female recruit's vagina to see if her hymen is still intact. If it is not, she is not eligible for military service. This is still going on in 2021! And for military service, not just to determine a woman's worthiness for a good marriage match.

Women have always been punished for having sex, wanting sex, enjoying sex. Why is this? Why does it both excite men and frighten them if a woman is sexually "aggressive?" Writing for *The Cut*, fittingly for the "Mating Behavior" section, Ann Friedman asserts, "Women like having sex. They don't like being socially punished for it." Research cited in this article shows that women are most turned on by their partners' desire for them. Women enjoy sex and they enjoy sex with people who really want them. The irony is that most straight men find it a turnoff when women are sexual aggressors. Consequently, women who pursue what they want (i.e., sex) don't get it. This goes against the common philosophy that men will have sex with any woman if given the opportunity. Then there's the complication that women are labeled as "sluts" if they actively pursue sexual relationships.

Personally, I think this leads to a lot of the date rape situations. The evidence is anecdotal for this, but I think I can make a case. Women assertively pursue their own sexual pleasure, and this makes men feel insecure. The more insecure men feel, the more their need to dominate the female personality exists. This leads to men forcing their sexual attentions onto women and blaming them for "wanting it" or "asking for it" when women are advocates for their own sexual pleasure. Women are supposed to be sexy, but not sexual or only sexual behind closed doors within a monogamous relationship. "A lady on the streets, but a freak in the sheets." How many times have we heard that statement or ones like it? Why can't I be a freak in both places if I want to without these weird social labels being slapped on me?

I read someplace that women need twice the affection, attention, and love to feel the same level of happiness as a man due to the serotonin/dopamine cycle in the brain. This makes so much sense to me. How often do women fish for compliments? Why do women dress up to impress their partners? This is all to get that extra affection. This is why a man outside the relationship flirting with a woman can alter her feelings of sexual attractiveness so powerfully. And I think it's the reason that women so easily get manipulated in relationships. There are more con men who prey on women than there are con women who prey on men. Again, some of this is anecdotal, but I think I'm on to something.

Women have been physically punished for wanting rights as simple as voting. In fact, there is a notorious incident that occurred on November 10, 1917, in which thirty-three suffragists from the National Woman's Party were arrested for picketing outside the White House. The male guards did not treat the women with respect or kindness. Women were manacled to the bars of their cells and forced to stand all night, had their arms twisted behind their backs and were slammed over iron benches, thrown into cells where they smashed their heads on the iron beds, knocking them out. This is known as the "Night of Terror."

So, lest we think that bad treatment for women was just part of ancient culture, let's remember, this was only a century ago, not that long in the span of time that humanity has been on this planet. Yet these women were tortured and beaten just for wanting to vote, for their opinion to matter as much as a man's. Let's keep in mind that even slaves and ex-slaves had been allowed to vote, so women were considered even lower class than blacks, which should add some perspective.

On the topic of slavery, let's talk about female slavery. In the ancient past and the not-so-ancient past, slaves have been expected to be sexually active as part of their duties. It's a virtual certainty that the only way you could get in trouble sleeping with a female slave was if she was owned by somebody else and you didn't ask permission first. It still wouldn't be considered rape; it was "property damage". Women with some jobs (prostitutes, waitresses, actresses) in ancient history were probably not allowed to file rape charges. They would have been treated as willing participants of the sex forced upon them because of the nature of their jobs. If they displayed their body or acted flirtatiously as part of their jobs, then clearly, they wanted to have a man's attention forced on them. (How often do we see this theme repeated in "show business?")

In the Middle Ages, St. Augustine was actually considered a progressive (massive eye-roll here) for stating in several of his treatises that raped women didn't need to kill themselves because they shared no blame in the act. However, even he suggested that some women enjoyed the act of forcible sex. He was rather fixated on the concept of "involuntary lust," which led him to advocate for celibacy.

Even free women didn't have it much better. 'Bride kidnapping' is still known to occur in very rural nations. In this scenario, young women are forcibly abducted, becoming unwilling brides. A recent article (dated June 2021) states that 'bride kidnapping' is still very much a problem in Kyrgyzstan. This appalling act that, by its very nature defines "rape culture" occurs in some parts of Africa, Asia, Mexico, and even Europe. Even the *Bible* relates stories of men killing entire villages and taking the virgin women as wives; of course, their virginity would likely have been verified by inspecting their hymens.

While back on the topic of virginity, it might bear reminding that not all women have hymens that are intact, whether they've had sex or not. Mama Doctor Jones, on her YouTube channel, has a fantastic video on this very topic that is worth watching. The hymen can either not form or be ruptured by other means. For some women, the hymen is a thicker tissue than for others. How many women were falsely accused of being "impure" on their wedding night simply because they didn't have a hymen or theirs wasn't intact due to some other physical change?

We like to think children were the only ones in the past who were to be "seen and not heard," but women were treated this way in many ancient cultures. In ancient Greece and Rome, women couldn't leave the home without a male escort, and when company came over, they weren't allowed to speak or to sit down for dinner. Women were to retire to their rooms, out of sight, because the presence of a woman could "bother" the men. Here, the word "bother" could be interpreted in many ways. One could interpret that as being simply annoying or to "bothering" of a sexual nature. Either way, women weren't even second-class citizens.

In the Middle Ages, in Europe, "unruly" women who openly expressed their anger could end up locked into a device called a shrew's fiddle. A shrew's fiddle was a wooden device (a trap) that was shaped similarly to a violin. It bound the woman's hands and face. Then the woman would be publicly shamed for showing anger by being led up and down the streets for bystanders to observe. There is also a device called the "scold's bridle." This was a metal mask with sharp teeth that had a bell attached. The bell was to draw attention, so bystanders could come and mock the woman.

Of course, adultery was severely punished. Many women were killed outright for this crime. Men were encouraged to have extra-marital affairs because men were known to be sexual creatures. In medieval times, they employed a rather decadent device known as the "breast ripper" that was used on women who were caught in the act of adultery and, likely, sometimes hadn't even committed the act, but were suspected of it. The use of the breast ripper wasn't just relegated to adultery. Sometimes miscarriages would be punished (yes, punished) by sentencing to the breast ripper.

Then, and fairly minor comparison, there are all the spectacular scientific discoveries made by women that were attributed to men. Let's take a look at some of these. Vera Rubin confirmed the existence of dark mater, working with Kent Ford in the 1960s and 1970s. Dr. Grace Murray Hopper created the first compiler tools for computer language. These tools were used to program the Harvard Mark I computer that was used during World War II. History notes that John von Neumann created the computer's first program, but Dr. Hopper invented the codes to program it. Esther Lederberg collaborated with her husband Joshua on microbial genetics, but she was the one who discovered lambda phage, which is a virus that infects E. coli bacteria. Her husband was awarded the 1958 Nobel Price for Physiology or Medicine for his discoveries. Esther's work was never recognized, though it was just as valuable. Jocelyn Bell Burnell took her discovery of irregular radio pulses to her advisor at Cambridge which led to a discovery of pulsars. Burnell got no credit for her discovery. Her advisor Anthony Hewish and another male on the team, Martin Ryle, received the Nobel Prize for Physics in 1974.

Women have been tortured, demeaned, raped, and been shown in no uncertain terms that their brains aren't worth recognizing. Sadly, in many countries, even in the United States, some of this behavior still occurs. Women just want a seat at the table. We want to be taken seriously. So, when you tell women that things like withholding abortions are about killing babies, not about a woman's right to her own bodily functions, how do you think we're supposed to feel?

Men are very lucky that women are not literally up in arms. Women could take back their power by force if they wanted to. In fact, I think some of the recent acts of violence against men by women are part of the pendulum swinging back the other way. I think things will get worse before they get better. More Lorena Bobbits will be in the news as women take this vast history of violence and hatred against women and channel it into their own violence and hatred against men.

SELF

RADIOACTIVE HEART

*"An exchange of empathy provides an entry point for
a lot of people to see what healing feels like."*

—*Tarana Burke*

TODAY, I POSSESS a sizeable amount of power. I'm at the forefront
of an industry that is gaining momentum as the most environmen-
tally friendly source of base-load electricity available to the world.
Experts are saying there is no going back to a pre-solar and wind
power existence. I'm married to a marvelous man, and we now live
in the house that we dreamed up and financed together. I mentor
my sisters and nieces (and they mentor me!).

I could also write a declaration of striking fragilities that make
my heart faint when I reflect on them. The power glass, the mirror,
is in front of me, allowing me to be multidimensional for sure, but
I'm working on serious frailties like body image and intimacy.

The power glass is also before you. Life fluctuates between
ecstasy and agony, wins and losses, ups and downs...... power and
fragility. I hope I've inspired you to think about your list. It may
be the here and now and then gone tomorrow with a significant
life event, whether it be triumphant or tragic. Your power load will
fluctuate.

There is power in declaration. I am a female engineer, but that
is not all that I am. I am a rape survivor. I am a woman who has
lost a friend to suicide. I am a sister. I am a wife. I am an aunt. I

am a person. I do not identify myself by my career or my gender. I cannot say, though, that my gender has not, as a result of the experiences that I have had, influenced my current identity.

The most defining aspect of my life has been my rape. I wish I could say that that wasn't true, but it would be a lie. I didn't realize how much it impacted me until quite recently. But it influences so much of my life, my choices, how I deal with others. It's like a cloak that I can't cast off. I feel like I wear it constantly and that people see it, even if I don't talk about it. I feel like people see that I am damaged, fragile, that I don't belong among the healthy women.

Rape made me a stronger person. How can you not survive that, survive the legal aftermath without being strong (though I certainly didn't feel strong at the time)? Simultaneously, it has made me fragile. Because of that experience, I have a hard time trusting. I don't trust that friendship is real, that I can open up to a person and show them the real me without that person realizing the truth: that I am unlovable. My rape demonstrated my unlovability to me in several ways. It showed me that I was not deserving of real, genuine, sexual interest and love from a man—only domination and humiliation. It showed me I was not deserving of love and friendship from the people in my life who had claimed the title of "friend." It showed me that I was not deserving of love from my youngest sister.

Rape made me reluctant to speak about personal issues. I learned that I could not speak to my friends or family about what had happened to me. My friends just didn't want to hear it because they didn't believe that it was rape. They thought I had "buyer's remorse," regretting a sexual experience the morning after. I know about buyer's remorse. I had that with the boy I had my first sexual experience with, and I had that with Melvin. This was not buyer's remorse. This was a forcible sex act. The problem is, the act didn't come with a beating, a stabbing, any vaginal trauma. So, like every other act of date rape, it was a "he said, she said" event.

It is virtually impossible for me to maintain a normal

relationship with anyone. With my husband, our first months of dating were quite hard. I was always afraid that he was going to decide I wasn't worth being with. I couldn't discuss the rape with him. It wasn't until much later that I was able to. And even then, I wasn't able to really open up about it. He doesn't like to hear about it. I don't really blame him. Not like I wanted it to happen to begin with. I like to think that his discomfort has to do with knowing I was really hurt, really damaged, by someone and that he can't do anything about it. But I think his discomfort is deeper. It's clearly not something we will be able to explore without counseling.

As I said in an earlier piece, there were times when my husband and I had sex that he would be too enthusiastic or too passionate and I would have flashbacks. I would cry. He didn't understand. How could he?

I can't have a normal friendship, either. I can't open up and be vulnerable. After all, if people realize how damaged I am, they might withdraw their friendship like my friends twenty years ago. Friendships with men are especially tricky. If they are very nice to me and want to pursue something more than just a casual "hang out as a group" type friendship, I can misunderstand their interest. I can either withdraw, thinking they are interested in "taking advantage" or, more likely, I can misinterpret their care for romantic love or attraction to me. This seems counter-intuitive, but I've come to realize that the misinterpretation is due to wanting a man to legitimately be attracted to me. Not to want to dominate me. I want a man to realize how smart, funny, and witty I am and to desire me for it.

I understand why women become promiscuous after a rape. It's sometimes because a woman is desperate to prove to herself that she is still desirable, that she is not "damaged goods." Other times, it is because a woman figures since she is damaged goods, then there's no point in not having sex with the men she meets. Then there is the desire to assert control over one's body and emotions. Rape survivors experience their rape as a loss of control, so some women attempt to retain control by taking on multiple lovers instead of becoming too attached to one individual. They move from sexual partner to sexual partner to avoid rejection. Some rape survivors use the experience of an orgasm or even the attention of a man to soothe the damaged self-esteem that is a primary side-effect of the rape. The euphoria produced by a man's flirtation or even the sexual act itself can psychologically relieve the pain from the assault.

I can be a very needy friend once I have found a friend to whom I can truly open up and show all my damaged pieces. If I feel ignored or like my friend doesn't have time for me, it hurts me disproportionately because of the loss of friendship I experienced before. I can also test friendships and other relationships to make sure the interest is truly real. I realize that I do this. I will say things and do things to "shock" someone who is starting to show true interest in me. It's a test to see if they will keep being my friend despite my bad behavior. Ultimately, when they decide I'm too much to deal with, it reaffirms my "un-lovableness." I will also offer up some truly deep emotional shit to see if they can continue to deal with it. The more they show they can, the harder I'll cling to them.

I tend to also feel like a burden to people. I feel like my shit is heavy and that I shouldn't ask them to take on any of it. I feel like my shit makes me unlovable, that the fact that I am damaged and fragile makes me a burden because I do need to talk about it. I do need to get it out. So again, the more someone shows me that they can be there for me, the more I will need that reassurance.

My experience with rape is why I keep my hair short. I like it short and feel more attractive, but that's just a bonus. Long hair can be used as a handle to hold one captive during rape. In my case, it was used to force my head down into my rapist's lap so that he could forcibly sodomize me. My hair was down to the middle of my back before my rape. Shortly thereafter, I had it chopped to almost a pixie. It hasn't been longer than a bob (and that cut was quite short-lived) since.

My rape is also why I actively accept being overweight. I don't overeat. I splurge on pizza maybe once a month and when I eat out, I still tend to eat fairly well. But being overweight means less attention from men. Most men like slender frames. If I am plus-sized, then the attention I get is "real" attention that is safe and personality- and wit-focused, at least in my mind. If a man is interested in me for my personality, then he's not interested in dominating me perhaps. I also know that physical appearance has nothing to do with rape. Rape happens to short women, tall women, old women, young women, skinny women, and fat women. A man who hates women will rape a woman if he has the opportunity, regardless of her appearance. I expose my own thin sense of psychological safety here to demonstrate the complicating thoughts and emotions that hold hands with trauma.

You would think being an engineer that my smarts are all that matters to me and that I don't look in the mirror and judge myself or look at the women surrounding me and judge myself. And how does that judgment fall out? It's always that I find myself lacking. I often feel fat and stupid. Most of that is internal dialogue that I have to control, but it doesn't help that we uphold a society that punishes women for being smarter than their male peers and for being overweight when the standard is supermodel thin. I remind myself when I look in the mirror that I am beautiful both inside *and* outside. I remind myself that I am loved by myself and by others. I remind myself that I am the one people feel comfortable coming to discuss their problems. That's a high compliment, and not one that people would give me if they didn't consider me worthy. But worthiness has to be defined from within. I work at it.

My biggest challenge right now is in our lovely new house. The master bathroom boasts a giant shower with a glass wall and door. It is directly across from the master bath double vanity. What this means is that for the first time ever, I can see my naked body in the bathroom mirror as I shower. It's a constant reminder that where I would love to have soft curves, I have rolls. That where I would love to see firm muscle, I see flab. That where I would like to see smooth skin, I see dimples and not the cute ones in your tush or your cheek, but the ones associated with cellulite. Every day, when I shower and catch sight of myself, it is a moment for me to stop and look at my body, to look myself in the eyes and say, "God didn't create you by accident. Regardless of your weight, you are special, and you have a purpose." I know deep down that I will never lose the weight until I learn to love my body as it is. This is some of the hardest work I've ever done. Harder, even, than recovering from rape. But I did that, so I can do this, too.

All of this is complicated by the fact that I feel things very deeply. I experience emotions very strongly. When I am angry, I am nearly enraged. I experience emotional pain quite severely. A lot of things make me cry: St Jude's commercials, ASPCA commercials, most movies about animals, and sweet cards from my husband. It makes it difficult not to internalize my experience with rape, not to mull it over and over.

My experience with a friend committing suicide also affected me very strongly. He was in graduate school in the physics program with me. He was Indian and gay. Not a combination that was well accepted by his family and their traditional culture. He was one of the sweetest people I ever knew. He invited me and two of my sisters, who he had never met before, over to his and his partner's apartment where they cooked dinner for us. Sadly, shortly after this dinner, his partner cleared out his bank account to pay for a drug problem. I think he knew his partner had a drug problem, but he didn't want to acknowledge it (there is a difference between knowledge and acknowledgement).

He went to his mother for comfort. His mother gave him to believe that his problems were a result of his lifestyle. He started talking about suicide shortly thereafter. He talked about buying a gun. I never took it seriously. A few days later, the physics department called a gathering of all the students (it was a small department at that time) and announced his death. The police had contacted one of the professors as his emergency contact. The police asked for someone to go identify the body, and a good friend of mine volunteered to do so. He had jumped off the roof of his building.

I was devastated. I thought it was my fault. That there was something I could have done, should have done to recognize how bad his mental state was and how close he was to actually killing himself. I realize now that this is a burden I should not have put on myself, but I think it's a version of survivor's guilt. That event deposited a deep sympathy in me for people who are made to feel like they don't belong. It took me a long time to get over it.

These events have defined me in ways I consider both strengths and weaknesses. I am more empathetic to others than I would have been otherwise. But I am damaged. I carry searing scars that may never completely heal. I struggle with that damage. I struggle to feel normal to feel wanted and worthy. Self-worth was an issue for me before my rape, but the rape itself proved to me my unworthiness. It is a vicious cycle and is painstaking to undo any of the damage.

I was lucky, recently, to make a good friend, who showed me that I could be vulnerable, be needy, even, and still be valued. My friendship with him has not been easy for me. Every time I show him a new emotional scar, I worry he will run away from our friendship. So far, he has not! In fact, he has gone out of his way to show me that even though I am damaged, I am still worthy of affection and friendship. It is still hard for me. Every time I message him on Facebook Messenger and see the checkmark showing my message has been sent and not read, I feel I am being ignored deliberately. If he doesn't respond, I think he's finally decided that I'm not worthy of his friendship anymore.

I wish I didn't feel this way. I wish I didn't need him to constantly prove his friendship for me. It makes me feel like such a burden. As I said before, I can be a needy friend. But he rises to the occasion every time. Every time he reminds me that I am awesome that I am deserving that he enjoys my friendship. I don't know why he does this. I have to test his patience. I am so grateful for his friendship. In a way it feels like I am being disloyal to my husband, but the topics I discuss in this book aren't always ones I can discuss with Gene. (I see you reading, Gene!)

Sadly, since I initially wrote this piece, the good friend I alluded to above is no longer a friend. After months of encouragement, telling me to share my hurt and struggles, to vent my frustration and anger, our friendship terminated in a very abrupt manner. I still don't really know what happened. Perhaps he finally realized what he was committing to.

He slowly became unavailable, ghosting me, while still sending me occasional messages that I should continue to share, that he was a shoulder to lean on. Perhaps I missed some warning signs that he wasn't on the same page as I was, like the voyeuristic "Feel free to keep sharing. I am learning a lot," and the "The wife is in a mood," when I inquired about his plans to attend my fortieth birthday party. Going back over the friendship, I have questioned my ability to read people and even my very sanity.

The worst part was when he told me that he'd realized I was "emotionally fragile" when I told him I was tired of feeling jerked around. It was like a slap in the face after he told me so many times and in so many ways that he was a safe place to land. How could I have been so wrong about him?

We seldom talk about the effects of a friendship breakup. How that can hurt worse than losing a romantic partner. If someone doesn't want to be your friend anymore, it's hurtful in a way that losing a romantic partner isn't. One can grow apart from a romantic partner, and there is typically a period of trying to work through things. When someone doesn't want to be your friend anymore it sends a different message.

That you are both unlovable and unlikable. As Jessica Pan says in her book, Sorry I'm Late, I Didn't Want to Come, *when someone doesn't want to be your friend the message is patently clear. You're not worth even liking. There's seldom a conversation to rehash why the friendship terminated. There's no "closure," typically. It's just over and you're left sitting there and wondering "What did I do to suddenly deserve being literally un-friended?"*

The "breakup" took place right after my fortieth birthday, so there was no way for that sense of "unworthy" to get wrapped up into the mid-life crisis that often follows turning forty, especially for women. The fact that I'd shared so much with him and been encouraged to do so led me to feel strung along and somewhat manipulated. Declaring this fragility will perhaps exorcise the emotions and thoughts still roiling through my brain.

LYRICAL RELEASE

*"Poetry is a mirror which makes beautiful
that which is distorted."*

—PERCY BYSSHE SHELLEY

I'VE NEVER HAD a particular interest in writing poetry. I've enjoyed reading Frost, Elizabeth Barrett Browning, Maya Angelou, and others, but then something miraculous happened. The need for lyrical release. Could expression be the ultimate key to power?

Solace in Social Media

I write
I write to find solace
To find solace from the pain
I write
To explain
To explain how I feel
Why I feel what I feel
To heal
To heal the pain
So I can truly feel again
So that I can love again
So that I can trust again

I write
And others respond
They respond to my posts
These hosts
These hosts of opinions
So many opinions
But none of them know
None know what I feel
None know how I struggle
I try to explain
Yet my efforts fall flat
Like words on a page
I can't ever explain my rage
This rage that consumes me
That buries me 'live
That wraps its tendrils around and within me
That causes me to hate
Hate myself
Hate the men
Hate the maleness within them
Hate their very anatomy
Yet I love them
I still love them
I just want them to understand
So I continue to write
I write to find solace
One day, solace from the pain

What He Took

He took my trust
My trust in men
My trust in humanity

My trust in friendship

He took my body
My body of proof
My body of truth
My body of justice

He took my faith
My faith in God
My faith in love
My faith in myself

He took my honor
My good name
My good fortune
My good word

I let him take these things from me
These things of intangibility
Not because I was soft or weak
But because I refused, out of fear, to speak
I let my fear, my shame, my youth
Keep me from speaking out my truth

I choose now to take these things back
To reclaim these things that I feel I lack
And now, at last, finally, at length
To reclaim, recoup, recapture my strength
To speak out, to say hard things, to be free
To take back that sparkling girl who is me

What He Did

Because of the thing that HE did
I withdrew into myself, I hid
I hid the sparkling girl within
For fear I had taken on the sin
That I was the one, the one to blame
That I should feel, somehow, the shame
That I was undeserving of
A decent and proper kind of love
That it was me, my lack of grace
That led to this horrible disgrace
And so I hid, I hid myself
I put my heart on a kind of shelf
And I decided that I would keep
My true self buried; buried deep
That I would never talk about
That night that left me filled with doubt
Doubt about my very worth
Worth that was ordained at birth
That night that made me disbelieve
(That pain I never could relieve)
Fear that I would be always scarred
By a man who had no heart
That my body would forever remember
The invasion of his thrusting member
The memory played like a tape
The memory… of my rape
But then I met a man named Jim
And so grateful that I am to him
For showing me so patiently
For helping me to view, to see
For helping me to realize

For letting me see me through his eyes
That I was not what was done to me
That I could speak, I could be free
That I could exercise my choice
I found my calling, I found my voice
I had to speak, I had to write
The verses spoke to me day and night
I could not rest, I could not think
Sometimes they brought me to the brink
The emotions writhing deep inside
No longer content to seethe and hide
A story I thought I could never tell
That I could never from the rooftops yell
A story that is filled with pain
A story I never thought I would tell again
But now I tell it not in hopes
That justice will bind HIM in its ropes
No, I tell it because, because I want
To no more let it my mind haunt
And now that I can speak, I see
That I can finally be free
That I can be free of his cock, his cum
And if I can be free, then so can some
Of the other women who relive in the night
Who relive the ultimate female fright
And maybe they can one day feel
Affection that is truly real
Friendship from a man like Jim
That can help to heal what was done by "him"
When Jim called me "brave," that simple word
A strange association, I never heard
That word in my mind, associated with this deed
But so very greatly did I need

To embrace that word, to make it mine
To drink it in like a glass of wine
So finally, I could tell my story
And finally, not feel the worry
And no longer because of the thing he did
Feel my specialness should be hid

Damaged

I was broken
But I am stronger
When my pieces came back together
They knitted more tightly
I am damaged
But I am also perfect
Perfect because I have resilience
Resilience keeps me fighting
I was hurt
But I am healing
It takes time to heal one's self
Healing is not easy
I was raped
But I am not a victim
Not a victim, but a survivor
A survivor is strong
I was damaged
But I reclaimed my power

Promises

He said I was "brave," but that was a word
That in my mind I had never heard
How could I be brave? My mind had said

When I had let him take me on my bed
When I had let him dominate me
When I had let him fuck me, rape me
He said he was honored that I would share
Would tell him things that laid me bare
He was honored to be my confidant
He said to vent to share whenever I want
But then the tide had turned, it seemed
And in that turn, I'd never dreamed
He'd be so cruel with his words his deeds
When he determined he couldn't meet my needs
Then he used a hurtful phrase
Words that sent me spiraling into a maze
A maze of self-doubt that was a cage
And filled me with the deepest rage
He said that I was "emotionally fragile"
I see myself as "emotionally agile"
How else would I have survived so long?
How else would I have become so strong?
I still don't know why he responded so
I guess that I will never know
He encouraged me to share to vent
And then with that one phrase he went
And destroyed any trust I had in him
And that's how I lost my friend named Jim

REFERENCES

Arlington Public Library. "This Week in 19th Amendment History: The Night of Terror."
https://library.arlingtonva.us/2019/11/12/
this-week-in-19th-amendment-history-the-night-of-terror/

Bates, Laura. *Everyday Sexism.* New York, New York: Simon and Schuster, 2015.

Bedford, Nicole. "Bride Kidnapping: A Shocking Rape Culture Tradition that's Still Happening." *Farewell Alarms.* November 12, 2018.
https://farewellalarms.com/bride-kidnapping-a-shocking-rape-culture-tradition-thats-still-happening-2ebe4a0bd880

Cahya, Gemma Holliani. "Indonesia army signals end to 'virginity test' for female recruits." *The Guardian.* August 5, 2021.
https://www.theguardian.com/world/2021/aug/06/
indonesia-army-signals-end-to-virginity-test-for-female-recruits

Chemaly, Soraya. *Rage Becomes Her.* New York, New York: Atria Books, 2019.

Chi, Guangqing, and Erin Hofmann. "'Bride kidnapping' haunts rural Kyrgyzstan, causing young women to flee their homeland." *MSN.com.* June 7, 2021.
https://www.msn.com/en-us/news/world/
bride-kidnapping-haunts-rural-*kyrgyzstan-*
causing-young-women-to-flee-their-homeland/
ar-AAKN2zl

Christiansen, Dorte, Rikke Bak, and Ask Elklit. "Secondary victims of rape." National Library of Medicine/PubMed.gov. 2012;27(2):246-62.doi: 10.1891/0886-6708.27.2.246.

https://pubmed.ncbi.nlm.nih.gov/22594219/

Clance, P. R., & Imes, S. A. "The imposter phenomenon in high achieving women: Dynamics and therapeutic intervention." *Psychotherapy: Theory, Research & Practice*, 15(3), 241–247. 1978. *https://doi.org/10.1037/h0086006*

Davies, Emma. "Nuclear power 'the only substitute for coal', expert says." *Stockhead.* July 6, 2021. *https://stockhead.com.au/energy/ nuclear-power-the-only-substitute-for-coal-expert-says/*

Friedman, Ann. "When Women Pursue Sex, Even Men Don't Get It." *The Cut.* June 4, 2013. *https://www.thecut.com/2013/06/when-women-pursue-sex-even-men-dont-get-it.html*

Kennedy, Pagan. "The Rape Kit's Secret History." *The New York Times.* June 20, 2020. *https://www.nytimes.com/interactive/2020/06/17/opinion/rape-kit-history.html*

Kleyman, Katia. "Horrible Torture Methods That Have Been Used Primarily on Women." *Ranker.* June 21, 2021. *https://www.ranker.com/list/torture-used-on-women-in-history/ katia-kleyman*

Lipman, Joanne. *That's What She Said.* New York, New York: William Morrow Paperbacks, 2019.

Maryland Coalition Against Sexual Assault. *https://mcasa.org/take-action/for-friends-family-of-survivors*

Miller, Rick. "What Is Power, Really?" *Forbes.* October 25, 2018. *https://www.forbes.com/sites/rickmiller/2018/10/25/ what-is-power-really/?sh=75b207ed42a7*

Oliver, Mark. "10 Horrible Realities Of Being A Woman Throughout History." *Listverse.* November 29, 2016. *https://listverse.com/2016/11/29/10-horrible-realities-of-being-a-woman-throughout-history/*

PBS. "The Roman Empire in the First Century."
http://www.pbs.org/empires/romans/empire/family.html

RAINN. "Sexual Violence Statistics."
https://www.rainn.org/statistics

Shumilova, Daria, and Irena Chatzis. "Not Your Typical Nuclear
Engineer: Blazing a Trail for Women." IAEA. March 6, 2020.
https://www.iaea.org/newscenter/news/
not-your-typical-nuclear-engineer-blazing-a-trail-for-women

Tasca, Cecilia, Mariangela Rapetti, Mauro Giovanni Carta, and
Bianca Fadda.

"Women And Hysteria In The History Of Mental Health." *Clin*
Pract Epidemiol

Ment Health. 2012; 8: 110–119. Published online 2012 Oct 19.
doi:

10.2174/1745017901208010110
https://www.ncbi.nlm.nih.gov/pmc/articles/PMC3480686/

Viegas, Jennifer. "Infanticide Common in Roman Empire." *NBC*
News. May 5,

2011.
https://www.nbcnews.com/id/wbna42911813

Vogelstein, Rachel, and Erik Fliegauf. "Women's Power Index:
Find Out Where Women Lead—and Why It Matters." Coun-
cil on Foreign Relations. April 14, 2021.
https://www.cfr.org/blog/womens-power-index-find-out-where-
women-lead-and-why-it-matters

World Nuclear Association. "Nuclear-Powered Ships." Updated
June 2021.
https://www.world-nuclear.org/information-library/non-power-
nuclear-applications/transport/nuclear-powered-ships.aspx

ABOUT THE AUTHOR

Katherine "Karle" Cooper has spent 14 years in the nuclear industry, with experience in new nuclear plant design and operating unit design and high-profile programs, such as Vogtle Units 3 & 4, the North Anna Unit 3, and mPower. Her current position is as Nuclear Engineer III at Dominion. Katherine holds a Professional Engineering license in the state of Maryland. *Power Glass* is her debut as an author, and she is a dedicated thought leader on topics that advance gender parity in STEM.